THE REAL PERSPECTIVE

THE REAL PERSPECTIVE

SECRET INVESTMENTS YOUR FINANCIAL ADVISOR WON'T TELL YOU ABOUT

MIKE BROWN

LIONCREST
PUBLISHING

THE REAL PERSPECTIVE
Secret Investments Your Financial Advisor Won't Tell You About

ISBN 978-1-5445-1531-1 *Hardcover*
978-1-5445-1529-8 *Paperback*
978-1-5445-1530-4 *Ebook*

CONTENTS

FOREWORD

I was born in a shack with a dirt floor, adobe walls, straw roof, no electricity, and no running water. That was the beginning.

Now, you've probably guessed this was not in the United States of America. I was born in Brazil.

Soon after, my father moved away to another city named Eden. He rented a house. This was a major move for our family. By the time I was five or six years old, he purchased a small lot, and with the help of his friend from the Navy, he built a one-room building—again with a mud floor, as before. However, this shack was *his*. It was not rented, and later he was able to build a house that was closer to the center of Eden.

Our new home in Eden was built with a stone foundation,

brick walls, and a concrete floor. It had a bathroom and French tile roofing, and it became our home. This was when my understanding of "real" estate originated and, since I immigrated to America at the age of twenty, this understanding has been enlarged to the power of ten.

My early years impressed on me the importance of how to create value with real assets. This is most likely why I've never trusted Wall Street and the fancy financial advisors constantly competing for my business.

I'll never forget taking my young daughter to an empty field far from the city lights. I told her she was looking at gold. She looked at me with a puzzled face, and many questions followed. Later that day, I purchased the property and built an industrial complex with four warehouses near Washington Dulles Airport. It was a total of 34,200 square feet of industrial buildings at the cost of $1,600,000. Today's value is over $10,000,000.

It was the beginning of my investment life.

This is why I'm so excited to write this foreword and open investors' eyes to how I created wealth for my family with the investment strategies found in this book.

I first met Mike Brown over twenty years ago, during the purchase of a commercial real estate investment property. The property was a heavy industrial warehouse building with tons of upside. I was a member of a syndicated group of investors that acquired commercial real estate to build wealth. We simply put our money together and invested in properties. This time, however, Mike was on the other side of the negotiating table, and he was not my friend.

It was a long and tedious negotiation, and ultimately we paid $100,000 over the asking price. This experience enraged myself and my partners, and the thoughts of doubt crept into our heads. Had we overpaid and had we made a terrible mistake?

It turns out we made an excellent decision to move forward, and the property has appreciated and created incredible cash flows for our investment group. I thought: *Man, this Mike is something else. He's tough, and we need him on our side next time.* That's how Mike and I became friends.

Since those early years, I've relied on the financial counsel of Mike and his experience to successfully build wealth for my family using the techniques you'll read in this book. I've discussed with Mike and other investor friends about why you can't rely solely on traditional Wall Street investments to build generational wealth.

This book outlines a lot of the conversations we've enjoyed

together and how you can use our experiences to move forward with your financial life. With Mike as my advisor, we've made millions of dollars together and created wealth for my family. I've learned to follow "Mike's Laws" of investing and have built solid investments alongside my real estate holdings. But real estate will always be my favorite type of investment.

So, with that in mind, if anyone asks me why real estate remains a foundation in my investment philosophy, my answer is very simple: "I was able to make lots of money and had lots of fun doing it." The satisfaction of seeing your investment in REAL estate, the ability to walk over it, to live and work in the property, and most importantly to own it—nothing can compare to that.

Again, it is REAL estate, not a piece of paper in someone's hand with unlimited control.

I own it.

I control it.

I built it.

I see it in REAL time.

That is simply my humble opinion of what REAL estate

means to me and the difference of owning versus Wall Street stock market investment.

Nelson A. DeSouza
Builder, Investor, and American Citizen

INTRODUCTION

The personal finance and investment industry has exploded. According to Cerulli Associates, there are more than three hundred thousand financial advisors working in the United States today. But not all financial advisors are the same; they're not all good, they're not all knowledgeable, and they don't all have the investor's best interests in mind.

On the surface, managing money may seem uncomplicated; most financial advisors can explain the difference between a mutual fund and a REIT. But do these advisors know how true wealth is created and maintained? Or are they missing inside secrets to how the rich get richer?

0.1. TRUST THE EXPERTS—RIGHT?

Most people consider financial advisors to be experts—people who can take care of their money and grow it. And while in theory that may be correct, the practice is very different. Financial advisors are good people; they're just stuck looking at the financial world from an old perspective, and they're struggling to innovate. From my experience, a few issues with financial advisors do stick in my craw and handicap investors' ability to create wealth. Do you feel the same?

SIMPLE LACK OF COMMUNICATION

Our money and financial well-being is important. Annual review meetings are not enough. Clients don't want a "set it and forget it" relationship with their advisors.

SELLING JUST TO EARN A COMMISSION

Financial advisors face conflicts of interest when they are tempted to sell certain products that deliver higher commissions. We need financial advisors who act in the client's best interest and recommend investments best for the client's particular situation.

LACK OF TRANSPARENCY WHEN IT COMES TO FEES AND PERFORMANCE

Fees and performance can become hidden within confusing language and disclaimers. Financial advisors need to be honest about what they are charging as well as the fees within the investments themselves.

NOT PUTTING CLIENTS' NEEDS FIRST

Sometimes financial advisors are incentivized to sell new products and services pushed by their firms. Advisors need to remember all clients are unique and need tailored planning.

NOT THINKING OUTSIDE THE BOX

Financial advisors use financial software to scale their client base. Simple inputs provide financial advice from the software. Today's environment requires our advisors to be more creative, giving personalized solutions that achieve better results.

NOT COMFORTABLE BRINGING IN OUTSIDE EXPERTS

Financial advisors should not be threatened by collaborating with other experts such as CPAs, estate attorneys, or real estate and life insurance professionals.

PROMISING UNREASONABLE RETURNS

Advisors can't guarantee 12 percent returns on your investments. We need to understand these big returns are just not the norm on Wall Street these days.

There are some great financial advisors out there, but what worked in the past won't work anymore. As you'll learn in these chapters, investing in Wall Street can no longer guarantee the returns it once promised, and your money is being tied up in outdated investing practices, layers of fees, and a lack of transparency on how Wall Street works. If you're sitting there wondering, *How come the rich get richer but I don't?* then the simple answer is that you're doing it wrong. You've been *advised* to do it wrong. And that's why I wrote this book: so you can clear away the myths and fog surrounding investing and learn the one secret to how the rich consistently grow their money. And it's not through Wall Street.

0.2. HOW DO THE RICH GET RICHER?

In this book, we'll talk about the one investment strategy that is indispensable to creating and maintaining wealth: true asset allocation. This is how the rich get richer. Recently, Global Pension Asset Study revealed that high-net-worth investors with a net worth up to $3 million *diversify 22 percent of their portfolios into private commercial real estate.*[1] And the wealthier one becomes, the more one does it: high-net-worth individuals with more than $10 million in assets *diversify 46 percent of their portfolios into private commercial real estate.*

1 Simone Foxman, "Wealthy Investors Are Leaving Hedge Funds for Real Estate," Bloomberg.com, July 18, 2017, https://www.bloomberg.com/news/articles/2017-07-18/wealthy-investors-leaving-hedge-funds-seek-haven-in-real-estate.

It doesn't matter what your net worth is today; you don't need $10 million to learn from what is given in this book. All you need is a willingness to take back control of your money from financial advisors and to make your wealth work for you. Through discussion of private commercial real estate as an asset allocation strategy, we're going to shed light on a new breakthrough in financial planning that will increase your return on investment by more than three to five times what you're getting today and provide security and peace of mind without the ups and downs of Wall Street. We're going to let you in on the secret so you can start using these techniques in your investment strategy today.

So why are you going to listen to me?

My path is unique. Not only am I a financial advisor with one of the best-known investment banking companies in the world, but I've also been a founding partner in two private commercial real estate investment and development companies. I've had firsthand experience with the bias financial advisors have with alternative asset allocation and investments that put their clients at a disadvantage. In the next chapter, I'll explain my journey in depth and how it's brought me here. Each of the insights in this book is hard-earned, and they'll show you how to build generational wealth so that you and your family can be at peace for decades to come.

CHAPTER 1

THE EARLY YEARS

Back in the eighties, I was the Alex P. Keaton of the day (if you ever watched the popular TV show *Family Ties*). I devoured books on Wall Street and investing and dreamed of one day working on Wall Street. Posters of the New York Stock Exchange and tall skyscrapers lined my childhood bedroom walls, while my peers had *Baywatch* models and famous athletic heroes. You could find me at the local library checking out everything in the business section; I often wondered why anyone would read fictional stories! How was that going to help me achieve my goals and make me rich?

I jumped into competitive mock stock trading contests and started many entrepreneurial ventures to raise money to invest in stocks. It was the roaring eighties, and Wall Street was the place to be. But I'll never forget the day I came across a new book called *The Art of the Deal*, written by a guy named Donald J. Trump. *Wow,* I thought, *this commercial real estate thing sounds pretty exciting!* Those 384 pages of gilded gold became my go-to bible of a sort. What if I could be a Wall Street guy and also invest in commercial real estate? Who knew that one day this dream would become a reality.

My first big break came when a family friend introduced me to a commercial real estate developer and investor. He offered me an apprenticeship, and I jumped at the chance. I learned how to evaluate complex investment deals, construction management, structuring development opportunities, and learned how millionaire business people thought much differently than most of my friends.

Wall Street would have to wait. I was going all in on commercial real estate.

I'll never forget my first deal. I drove into a dusty industrial area hidden behind the airport and found a treasure. This was the ugliest piece of real estate you've ever seen. It was 4.3 acres of flat dirt located in a heavy industrial-zoned area that was the home to an aging crane construction company. To the untrained eye, it was a junkyard. But I'd been learning about zoning classifications and how it impacts real estate valuations. This was going to be great.

After meeting with the property owners, I quickly assembled a group of investors to buy the property. We did it, and we eventually sold the investment a year later for more than a 300 percent return. Walking out of that real estate closing one week before Christmas with a six-figure check was exhilarating. My Wall Street dreams took me to Main Street, and real estate was now my game.

I continued to invest alongside my clients and recruited other investors in a diverse collection of commercial real estate assets. We invested in office buildings, industrial and retail deals, along with acquiring land to position for new development. Over the years, I participated in more than $1 billion in transactions and learned from the best in the industry.

The next logical step in my commercial real estate career was to create an investment fund to pool investors and acquire properties to create long-term wealth. This gave us the opportunity to have the necessary funds to take advantage of deals immediately without having to raise capital once a deal was identified. It was interesting to begin hearing feedback from investors about real estate and the stock market. This is when it became apparent that wealthy investors preferred real assets and often only used Wall Street for small portions of their overall investment portfolio. Our investment funds not only provided steady income through dividends to our investors, but had huge upside with property appreciation. An investor friend described it like a CD bank coupon with a lottery ticket at the end.

Living in a high-growth market near Washington, DC, we found the deals were plentiful and we needed more investors to take advantage of the opportunity. To maintain the growth of our investment funds, it was necessary to reach out to financial advisors, independent wealth managers, and other traditional Wall Street players to see if their clients would like to invest in our real estate funds. This was a natural fit: financial advisors have clients who need to diversify and allocate real assets into their portfolios. It became apparent these guys had a different agenda: sell Wall Street products that fit nicely into their firm's platforms and collect fees no matter what happened to their clients' financial lives. These advisors agreed that we were offering excellent investment opportunities, but they were never willing to invest their clients' money. It's simple to see the conflict of interest. Fees and commissions are only paid on sanctioned firm investments. The advisors were never going to tell their clients about commercial real estate. This made me mad as hell. How could these guys, who are responsible for the well-being of their clients' wealth, be so blinded and irresponsible? Could I convince them to reconsider and put their clients' wealth ahead of their own personal agenda? It became an obsession to educate and convince the financial advisor community to rethink what they've been taught for years by Wall Street banks.

I spent countless months educating investment professionals with seminars, meetings, and proposals, only to fall on deaf ears. How could they not understand the power of true asset allocation that undoubtedly increased their clients' returns while protecting their exposure to volatile markets? The hard facts proved my point. But self-interest prevailed; the advisors had no interest in asset allocation for their clients and continued to do business as usual.

Have I stumbled upon an opportunity? If the status-quo financial advisors wouldn't entertain innovative investment allocation to help their clients, maybe I should dig deeper. I really needed to understand the mindset of the financial advisor and wealth management business to gain perspective on how these firms constructed investment portfolios and why they recommended specific investment choices to their clients.

What would any logical person do in such a situation? I took a leave of absence from my real estate business and joined the Merrill Lynch financial advisor trainee program. This may sound extreme, but I always wanted to work on Wall Street! You're probably thinking that I'm a bit crazy at this point, but if my passion was truly to build investment portfolios to beat Wall Street, it was only logical to learn from the inside why financial advisors do what they do. At the time, my commercial real estate partner was generous and continued to manage our business while I took a leave of absence to study and learn the wealth management business from the Wall Street perspective. It was important enough to take the time and learn valuable insights so I could give the highest level of advice to my investors.

I finally arrived on Wall Street.

It took four months of taking aptitude exams and having lengthy interview discussions on why an investment bank should hire a guy like me. But I finally prevailed and was hired into the Merrill Lynch program. It was exciting to join the "Rolling Herd," the nickname on Wall Street for Merrill advisors, and get this rare glimpse into what goes on in the inside. I was going to learn to be a classic stockbroker from the best in the business.

My first day, I walked into the fancy office building adorned with bull statues and marble. The fun ended there, when my new manager dropped the huge textbooks for my Series 7 exam on the desk and said, "Start studying." I had six months to study for and pass the infamous Series 7 and 66 security exams, or I would be fired on the spot. Studying gave me an excellent education on Wall Street products such as mutual funds, option trading, stock picks, and financial planning. It was interesting not finding much on real estate investing in these huge books. It became apparent that it wasn't the fault of the financial advisor regarding their lack of knowledge of real estate investments; Wall

Street firms simply didn't provide access to the products, so they had no interest in telling these young advisors about the subject. My Wall Street education was focused on sales and how to convince trusting investors on why they should purchase these investment products, as opposed to how to build a solid investment strategy for clients.

Fast-forward. I passed the exams and became an official licensed Merrill Lynch financial advisor. This was going to be great! Maybe it was my calling to build a wealth management practice that incorporated private commercial real estate and prove my investment philosophy to all the naysayers. Well, that dream didn't last long. My time at Merrill Lynch was sitting in a bullpen making four hundred cold calls a day. Our management didn't care one bit about the client; it was nothing but a quota shop and who could bring in the most money to the firm. There was no doubt: this was a sales job, and no one cared about the well-being of our clients' investments.

I was also quickly introduced to the term "selling away." "Selling away" meant that no financial advisor could introduce a client to an investment product outside of what the firm provided; it was forbidden and illegal. Basically, this was a slick rule that kept fees and client assets inside the firm's control without any concern for the well-being of the client. Not only was this completely unethical in my opinion, but the Wall Street investment model became crystal clear to me. Wall Street was only interested in capturing clients' assets and misleading them to alternative investment strategies available in the market.

Now there is much more to say on the subject and about my journey as a new financial advisor while actively managing a commercial real estate business. That's exactly why I wrote this book: to expose what's really happening inside the Wall Street investment business model and how it can dramatically impact your wealth.

I'm going to show you how this new experience helped my company create an entirely new discipline in financial wealth management. The world has become too complex to rely on financial advisors who see investments through a single lens. What you need is a team of diverse experts and practitioners working in full alignment with your best interests in mind, forging a partnership to bring optimal investment returns to you. It's a new day in financial planning, and this book will bring new perspective on how to properly allocate your investment portfolio for maximum return.

Along the way I'll give you "Mike's Laws" of investing that my team has developed over the years of commercial real estate investing and wealth management. These laws of investing have given me the discipline and guidance to predict a consistent and successful investing strategy. I've also

MIKE'S LAW #1

Asset Allocation

This is the most important of all the laws. Asset allocation is the single most important decision you will make as an investor. All investment portfolios must have proper division among different asset classes. Investors are often misinformed by their financial advisors that asset allocation is simply defined as diversification. Diversification is important, but diversifying an investment portfolio by holding an assortment of stocks and bonds does not equal true asset allocation. The best-performing investment portfolios built for the long term have an allocation strategy in other asset classes that don't involve traditional Wall Street products. These asset classes involve real estate and commodities along with stocks and bonds. Investors do not spend enough time or thought on asset allocation, which is required for success.

included a bonus chapter to help you evaluate your personal financial advisor and determine if they truly have your best interests in mind while giving you investment advice. At the very end, you'll have an easy glossary of terms that you can refer to if some words seem a bit foreign. You'll also have access to my contact information for questions and comments on information you've read. I'm here to help and assist you in any way possible.

My insights will give you an edge in avoiding common misunderstandings and mistakes; they're the kind only learned through experience. My unique experience opened my eyes to this new form of financial planning and asset allocation, and I'm excited to let you in on the secret. It's time to get started and take back control of our financial lives. Are you ready?

1.1. WHAT'S NEXT?

Over the next few chapters, I'm going to beat up on Wall Street and my traditional financial advisor friends. It's good therapy, and it has led to my breakthrough in investing. I'm going to show you how adding specific assets to your investment life will bring significant returns without the Wall Street effect.

If you take the simple steps explained in this book, it will bring you the peace of mind that your wealth will grow in a way you've never experienced. You're going to learn what true diversification means, not what the Wall Street marketing machine has been selling us for years. And you're going to learn that that's how the rich get richer: through this new approach in financial planning that emphasizes asset allocation.

I hope you're excited to get started. In the next chapter, we'll begin with the basics: we'll take an honest look at Wall Street and how it affects our money and future. Remember, it's *your* money. And it's time to know why your financial advisors do what they do.

KEY TAKEAWAYS

- → Investors today need more from their financial advisor. Wall Street alone can never deliver the returns needed to create and maintain wealth.
- → The secret investment strategy of the wealthy individuals can generate three to five times investment portfolio growth with its simple technique.
- → A bold new approach to wealth management is desperately needed in today's financial advisory business.
- → The Wall Street banks don't always have the investors' best interest. It's necessary for today's sophisticated investor to know the pitfalls often sold through Wall Street banks and how to protect their wealth.
- → Asset allocation is the only way to true investment portfolio diversification. Asset allocation is the most important decision an investor will make.
- → There is a huge difference between true asset allocation and what your financial advisor will sell you as asset allocation.
- → There are inherent conflicts of interest between financial advisors and other experts.
- → The rich do get richer using the techniques of asset allocation.

CHAPTER 2

WALL STREET IS NOT THE ONLY CHOICE

It's your money! It's time to step back and really think about your investing future. But let's first take a history lesson on Wall Street so we can really understand what's happening today in the financial advisory business. Are the financial experts really operating in your best interests? To answer that, you first need to know what your best interests may be. What do you want when it comes to investing? Better returns? Safety and security? Income? Transparency? At the time of this writing, we are deep into the COVID-19 pandemic that has sent the Wall Street markets on a ten-thousand-point roller coaster ride. This is more evidence of how unforeseen events can drastically affect your wealth and retirement future.

Henry Ford, one of America's greatest business innovators,

once said: "If I had asked people what they wanted, they would have said faster horses."

By saying this, Ford had no intention of belittling his customers. He just knew his customers didn't know how to articulate what they wanted or needed. Today's personal finance industry faces the same dilemma. One in three Americans have no idea what a financial advisor does, and that number increases to 46 percent among millennials.[2] Is this because the financial services industry hasn't kept up with the times to meet customer needs in the new economy? Perhaps. Do investors really know how to allocate their investment portfolios to maximize return? Where do they turn for advice, and can they rely on their financial advisor?

With the uncertainty of Wall Street and the tidal wave of financial advisors hunting for our dollars to manage, it may be time for a revolution on Wall Street and in the financial service industry. Investors need options, and this is exactly why I wrote this book. Henry Ford would see this: our investment lives need innovation, disruption, and new ideas to guarantee our wealth. This not only a safe strategy, but critical in growing wealth for our future and our family's future. Even if you don't agree, hear me out and I'll guarantee I'll leave you with fresh ideas for your investment strategy.

---

2 Deborah Nason, "Do You Know What a Financial Advisor Actually Does for a Living . . . or for You?," CNBC, June 21, 2016, https://finance.yahoo.com/news/know-financial-advisor-actually-does-115000422.html.

FUN FACT

Most people don't realize it, but McDonald's was never established as a hamburger restaurant chain. It's actually one of the world's best real estate portfolios. Former McDonald's CFO Harry J. Sonneborn said, "We are not technically in the food business. We are in the real estate business. The only reason we sell fifteen cent hamburgers is because they are the greatest producer of revenue, from which our tenants can pay us rent."

McDonald's owns $40 billion worth of real estate (before depreciation) with annual revenues of $9 billion, of which $4 billion is profit.

Franchisees flip burgers while McDonald's gets paid for owning commercial real estate all over the world.

But let's first take a walk down Wall Street and see how we got here.

2.1. TROUBLES ON WALL STREET

The S&P 500 and Dow Jones Industrial Average fell 6.2 percent and 5.6 percent in 2018. These were the largest annual losses since the Great Recession of 2008, when they fell 38.5 percent and 33.8 percent. The Nasdaq Composite lost 3.9 percent in 2018, the exchange's worst decade since it dropped 40 percent.

Question—did your phone ring just now with your financial advisor talking you off the ledge? "Don't worry, Mr. Investor, we're in the market for the long haul. The stock markets always come back strong and have consistently gained more than 8 percent annually for the past eighty years." When I was a financial advisor at Merrill Lynch, we were given these talking points by management on a regular basis when the market experienced hiccups. These talking points were nothing but sales tactics to keep clients in the market.

Well, to all the status-quo financial advisors out there, remember that in the hundred-year period between 1816 and 1914, Europe suffered no continent-wide war. Ladies and gentlemen, numbers lie and can be distorted anyway you like.

The other favorite talking point from financial advisors is the "magic of compound interest" and how they'll provide the inside track to 12 percent annual growth in the market. Now let's get serious: do you think we have access to these extraordinary money managers with the skills and resources to beat the market consistently? Of course not. The concept of compound interest is the most common misconception among investors. Financial advisors use the compound interest narrative to project future market earnings and convince you why Wall Street is a smart bet.

For example, between 1999 and 2018, the S&P 500 Index performed an average rate of return of 5.13 percent. The average investor would obviously think their wealth grew by 5.13 percent a year over the last twenty years. If you invested $100,000, then you'd have $258,776 according to the logic above. But you'd be wrong. Why? Because stock markets do not operate in a linear, straight line. Markets act like roller coasters with up and down years, and they never end up balancing out to a simple equation.

Here's the most critical point to investing on Wall Street. If you invested $100,000 in 1999 and cashed in your portfolio in 2018, your balance would actually be $203,911, which is over $50,000 less than what the market averages tell us.

Since stock markets fluctuate, when there is a loss, a subsequent gain must be much higher to balance out the loss. For example, if you lost 10 percent on your $100,000 investment, your balance would be $90,000. To make up this loss and break even, you would have to earn 11.1 percent, not 10 percent. If you lose 10 percent one year and then gain 10 percent the next year, your average return over the two years is 0 percent, but you have actually lost money. Using the $100,000 example, you are down to $90,000 after year one but only bounce back to $99,000 after a 10 percent gain in the second year, which leaves you $1,000 less than you started with.

Take a look at the chart below. This chart shows the actual returns on the $100,000 investment. The return is actually only 3.82 percent annually, and when you factor in the average fund manager fee of 1 percent, your balance erodes to $167,126 or a 2.75 percent return before taxes.

20 YEAR S&P INDEX FUND RETURNS $100,000 INITIALLY INVESTED WITH FEES

YEAR	STARTING BALANCE	EARNING RATE	INTEREST / EARNED	YEARLY MGT FEE	END OF YEAR ACCOUNT BALANCE	EARNING RATE AFTER FEES
2000	$100,000.00	-10.14%	$(10,140.00)	$(1,000.00)	$88,860.00	-11.14%
2001	$88,860.00	-13.04%	$(11,587.34)	$(888.60)	$76,384.06	-14.04%
2002	$76,384.06	-23.37%	$(17,850.95)	$(763.84)	$57,769.26	-24.37%
2003	$57,769.26	26.38%	$15,239.53	$(577.69)	$72,431.10	25.38%
2004	$72,431.10	8.99%	$6,511.56	$(724.31)	$78,218.35	7.99%
2005	$78,218.35	3.00%	$2,346.55	$(782.18)	$79,782.71	2.00%
2006	$79,782.71	13.62%	$10,866.41	$(797.83)	$89,851.29	12.62%
2007	$89,851.29	3.53%	$3,171.75	$(898.51)	$92,124.53	2.53%
2008	$92,124.53	-38.49%	$(35,458.73)	$(921.25)	$55,744.55	-39.49%
2009	$55,744.55	23.45%	$13,072.10	$(557.45)	$68,259.20	22.45%
2010	$68,259.20	12.78%	$8,723.53	$(682.59)	$76,300.14	11.78%
2011	$76,300.14	0.00%	$-	$(763.00)	$75,537.14	-1.00%
2012	$75,537.14	13.41%	$10,129.53	$(755.37)	$84,911.30	12.41%
2013	$84,911.30	29.60%	$25,133.74	$(849.11)	$109,195.93	28.60%
2014	$109,195.93	11.39%	$12,437.42	$(1,091.96)	$120,541.38	10.39%
2015	$120,541.38	-0.73%	$(879.95)	$(1,205.41)	$118,456.02	-1.73%
2016	$118,456.02	9.54%	$11,300.70	$(1,184.56)	$128,572.16	8.54%
2017	$128,572.16	19.42%	$24,968.71	$(1,285.72)	$152,255.15	18.42%
2018	$152,255.15	-6.24%	$(9,500.72)	$(1,522.55)	$141,231.88	-7.24%
2019	$141,231.88	28.88%	$40,787.77	$(1,412.32)	$180,607.33	27.88%
1Q 2020	$180,607.33	-20.00%	$(36,121.47)	$(1,806.07)	$142,679.79	-21.00%

Average Annual Return with Fees: 4.38%
Actual Annual Return with Fees: 1.77%
Actual ROI with Fees: 42.68%

Another favorite talking point is "dollar cost averaging." This concept is to ignore market fluctuations and consistently invest in the stock market with the same amount at the same time over and over. This concept was one of my favorites as a kid reading investment books. I'll never forget hanging out at the library reading books on Wall Street. It took real experience to learn the true concept of "dollar cost averaging."

If you invested $10,000 on an annual basis between 1999 and 2018 with an average 1 percent management fee, your ending balance would be $332,672.40, which is a 3.32 percent actual rate of return. Keep in mind that, in this example, you have invested $200,000 total.

20 YEAR S&P INDEX FUND RETURNS $100,000 INITIALLY INVESTED WITH FEES

YEAR	STARTING BALANCE	EARNING RATE	INTEREST / EARNED	YEARLY MGT FEE	END OF YEAR ACCOUNT BALANCE	EARNING RATE AFTER FEES
2000	$10,000.00	-10.14%	$(1,014.00)	$(100.00)	$8,886.00	-11.14%
2001	$18,886.00	-13.04%	$(2,462.73)	$(188.86)	$16,234.41	-14.04%
2002	$26,234.41	-23.37%	$(6,130.98)	$(262.34)	$19,841.08	-24.37%
2003	$29,841.08	26.38%	$7,872.08	$(298.41)	$37,414.75	25.38%
2004	$47,414.75	8.99%	$4,262.59	$(474.15)	$51,203.19	7.99%
2005	$61,203.19	3.00%	$1,836.10	$(612.03)	$62,427.25	2.00%
2006	$72,427.25	13.62%	$9,864.59	$(724.27)	$81,567.57	12.62%
2007	$91,567.57	3.53%	$3,232.34	$(915.68)	$93,884.23	2.53%
2008	$103,884.23	-38.49%	$(39,985.04)	$(1,038.84)	$62,860.35	-39.49%
2009	$72,860.35	23.45%	$17,085.75	$(728.60)	$89,217.49	22.45%
2010	$99,217.49	12.78%	$12,680.00	$(992.17)	$110,905.31	11.78%
2011	$120,905.31	0.00%	$-	$(1,209.05)	$119,696.26	-1.00%
2012	$129,696.26	13.41%	$17,392.27	$(1,296.96)	$145,791.57	12.41%
2013	$155,791.57	29.60%	$46,114.30	$(1,557.92)	$200,347.96	28.60%
2014	$210,347.96	11.39%	$23,958.63	$(2,103.48)	$232,203.11	10.39%
2015	$242,203.11	-0.73%	$(1,768.08)	$(2,422.03)	$238,012.99	-1.73%
2016	$248,012.99	9.54%	$23,660.44	$(2,480.13)	$269,193.30	8.54%
2017	$279,193.30	19.42%	$54,219.34	$(2,791.93)	$330,620.71	18.42%
2018	$340,620.71	-6.24%	$(21,254.73)	$(3,406.21)	$315,959.77	-7.24%
2019	$325,959.77	28.88%	$94,137.18	$(3,259.60)	$416,837.36	27.88%
1Q 2020	$426,837.36	-20.00%	$(85,367.47)	$(4,268.37)	$337,201.51	-21.00%

Total Invested: $210,000.00

Average Annual Return with Fees: 3.38%

Actual Annual Return with Fees: 2.37%

Actual ROI with Fees: 60.6%

Let's take one last look at Wall Street returns.

Imagine you invested $1,000 in the Dow Jones Average back in 1930. Can you imagine how much your portfolio would be worth today? The *Fox Business News* article by Erik Krom sums it up like this: "If you add up every number of the Dow Jones and divide it by 81 years, the returns average to 6.31 percent; however, if you do the math, you get an actual return of 4.31 percent. Your $1,000 investment in 1930 at 6.31 percent would grow to $142,000, but would actually be $30,000 at 4.31 percent." This does NOT calculate any advisor fees.[3]

After the Great Recession of 2008, I've become even more obsessed and focused on how to take back control of my money and help others in the process. If you don't control your wealth, then Wall Street will. There must be another way. This is why I am calling for a fresh approach to the financial services industry. Financial advisors do play an important part in our investment strategy, but a new way of business is needed.

During my research, I discovered a startling fact about affluent Americans. The number-one fear is not terrorism, healthcare, environmental concerns, or even death. The number-one fear according to a study conducted by

3 Erik Krom, "Solving the Myth of Rate of Return," *Fox Business News*, January 11, 2016, https://www.foxbusiness.com/features/solving-the-myth-of-rate-of-return.

Mass Mutual Insurance is the fear of outliving their savings. According to an Ernst and Young study: "75 percent of Americans can expect to see their assets disappear before they die."[4]

Now, we've all worked hard to build wealth. We've started businesses, we've practiced law and medicine, and we've invested and saved for our futures. So how did Wall Street become so powerful, and can we trust our future to the traditional paths of investing? My intention over the pages of this book is to create a dialogue to discuss the pitfalls of traditional Wall Street investing and to explore unique financial strategies that result in a solid plan to build and preserve wealth for your family and community.

"I sincerely believe that banking establishments are more dangerous than standing armies."

—THOMAS JEFFERSON

2.2. WHAT EXACTLY IS WALL STREET?

When we think of Wall Street, it's often the New York Stock Exchange and exciting images of the stock ticker flashing across our screen. But in reality, Wall Street is much bigger and affects our lives in many ways.

---

4 Peter Dizikes, "Study: Many Americans Die with 'Virtually No Financial Assets,'" *MIT News*, August 3, 2012, http://news.mit.edu/2012/end-of-life-financial-study-0803.

Wall Street is the financial business industry in a very broad and general sense. It's the investment banks, stock exchanges, stock brokerages, and investment companies. This group of players enjoys the most powerful influence in the world. Despite the scandals and stories of corruption, the roller-coaster ups and downs, the Wall Street players continue to grow in power and influence.

But how did Wall Street get control of our lives? If you don't understand the foundational basis of our history, it's difficult to move forward successfully.

2.3. HOW WALL STREET CREPT INTO OUR LIVES

Back in the *Leave It to Beaver* days of the late 1950s, less than 5 percent of Americans were invested in the stock market. That number quadrupled to one in five by the 1980s, and by the year 2000, more than 50 percent of Americans were invested in the stock market.

The financial and investment industry has exploded. CNBC, *Bloomberg*, and *Fox Business News* have become entertainment. There are financial advisor celebrities such as Suze Orman, Dave Ramsey, and Jim Cramer. Thousands of websites and apps are now providing up-to-the-minute financial advice. Did you know that one in four people will log on to a website, app, or financial planning program to assist in their investment lives?

So how did this happen?

It all started with a wonderful piece of tax code written in the early eighties that gave every American the opportunity to take their financial future into their own hands. This tax code created the 401(k) and is the primary source of saving for retirement today.

But here's the dirty little secret. The 401(k) was never intended to be a vehicle for retirement. That's right... And if not used correctly, the 401(k) can destroy your wealth.

The 401(k) was originally created to give business executives a place to put their big year-end bonuses. What eventually happened was a true "light bulb" epiphany. The executives now had a tool to transfer the costs and obligations of employee pensions *to their employees*; they could make it their employees' responsibility.

How? Let's quickly define the difference between a pension and a 401(k).

A pension is a contractual obligation between the company and the employee. This means the company accurately predicted the precise benefits required for each employee at retirement. In other words, it was a guaranteed financial plan for the employee with defined monthly benefits they would receive—a true contractual obligation.

Now this was not always carried out correctly or in the best interests of the employee. There are many instances where the company providing the pension either mismanaged funds or did not withhold sufficient funds for future benefits. Some high-profile companies such as American Airlines in 2005 and Bethlehem Steel in 2001 went bankrupt due to mismanaged pension funds.

The 401(k) became the modern replacement for the pension fund. The sizzle of the 401(k) was the opportunity to take our financial future back into our own hands. A strong bull market in the eighties contributed to the enthusiasm for this financial tool and marked it as clearly distinct from a boring, guaranteed pension fund. *Wall Street is going to make us rich!*—that was what was on the minds of working America. But in the excitement, we overlooked the fact that 401(k) plans didn't guarantee returns, fees, income, or the principal invested.

The simple creation of the 401(k) created the ultimate bull market of the eighties and nineties, with tons of cash moving into the hands of Wall Street. No longer was Wall Street an unattainable place, meant only for wealthy high-net-worth investors and savvy institutional players. It was now available to every American to build their retirement dreams.

So the party began...

A few obvious issues became apparent. What does the average American know about investing? For starters, according to the Employee Benefit Research Institute, almost half of working Americans have no clue as to how much money they'll need to retire.[5] The standard formula presented by most companies' 401(k) providers was simply to invest 5–10 percent of your paycheck into the fund and your wealth will grow accordingly. A Stanford economics professor, John Shoven, sums it up: "It's not realistic to finance a 30 year retirement with 30 years of work. You can't expect to put 10 percent of your income aside and then finance a retirement that's just as long."

An article in the *New York Times* by Teresa Ghilarducci painted the wealth-building challenge even more clearly. Here's an extract from the article:

> Not yet convinced that failure is baked into the voluntary, self-directed, commercially run retirement plan system? Consider what would have to happen for it to work for you. First, figure out when you and your spouse will be laid off or be too sick to work. Second, figure out when you will die. Third, understand that you need to save 7 percent of every dollar you earn. (Didn't start doing that when you were 25, and you are 55 now? Just save 30 percent of every dollar). Fourth,

5 Emily Brandon, "The Ideal Retirement Age, and Why You Won't Retire by Then," *U.S. News and World Report*, April 15, 2019, https://money.usnews.com/money/retirement/aging/articles/the-ideal-retirement-age-and-why-you-wont-retire-by-then.

> earn at least 3 percent above inflation on your investments, every year. (Easy, just find the best funds for the lowest price and have them optimally allocated). Fifth, do not withdraw any funds when you lose your job, have a health problem, get divorced, buy a house, or send a kid to college. Sixth, time your retirement account withdrawals so the last cent is spent the day you die.[6]

So where do most people put their money? Let's take a look at the most popular choices...

The most popular would be stock market index (ETF) and mutual funds, especially for 401(k) vehicles. And wow, there are plenty to choose from. According to Morningstar, there are now over 10,000 index and mutual funds and they're growing by the day.[7] This sounds like a good thing, but unfortunately this increases complexity for investors and causes paralysis by analysis. It also increases the chances for bad choices.

"Always mystify, mislead, and surprise."

—STONEWALL JACKSON

6 Mark Miller, "The Decade in Retirement: Wealthy Americans Move Further Ahead," *New York Times*, December 14, 2019, https://www.nytimes.com/2019/12/14/business/retirement-social-security-recession.html.

7 Statista, "Number of mutual funds in the United States from 1997 to 2018."

MIKE'S LAW #2

Control Your Own Destiny

"Control your own destiny or someone else will do it for you," said Jack Welch, the former CEO of General Electric.

No financial advisor cares about your money like you do. Investors must strive for financial independence to ensure security, choices, and opportunities. There are many factors we cannot control as investors, such as interest rates, stock markets, government policy, terrorist attacks, and economic cycles. History repeats itself. If investors listened once in a while, maybe history wouldn't repeat itself. As investors, we can buffer ourselves from these external factors by managing the things we have control over. We can control our debt levels, investing methods, and strategies and savings.

"Prepare for the unknown by studying how others in the past have coped with the unforeseeable and the unpredictable," explains the great General George S. Patton.

2.4. POPULAR WALL STREET PRODUCTS AND THEIR FAILINGS

In the United States alone, there is $15.02 trillion invested in mutual funds and more than $30 trillion invested worldwide. Does buying a professionally managed fund eliminate the need to buy individual stocks? Is it the best choice? Let me help: 96 percent of mutual funds failed to match or beat the market. Berkshire Hathaway, owned by the so-called greatest investor of all time, Mr. Warren Buffett, has failed to beat the S&P 500 since 2008.

I could write an entire book on the pitfalls of mutual fund

investing, but let's move to another popular investment choice: target-date funds. Target-date funds were created by Wall Street to "help" investors create automatic investing plans that take into account your investing plan and future date of retirement. This quickly became a fast-growing product on Wall Street. How much easier could it be? "Set it and forget it" was the pitch to investors.

A few examples of target-date funds: Barclays and Wells Fargo created the "LifePath" funds, while Fidelity offers "Fidelity Freedom." Basically, these funds allocate a percentage of bonds and equities in a schedule that employs a less risky allocation the closer to the targeted retirement date. The technique is often referred to as a "glide path." The funds invest in stocks (riskier) in the beginning years and move to a heavier allocation of bonds (less risky) near retirement. More than half of companies today use target-date funds for their employee retirement plans.

But here's the problem. Investors did not really understand what a target-date fund is and how it works. For example, a survey conducted by the Behavioral Research Associates found serious misconceptions among investors:

- 62 percent of investors thought they could retire when the target-date arrives.
- 30 percent of investors believed target-date funds had guaranteed returns.

- 57 percent of investors thought they would not lose any money in the fund.[8]

Big surprise—following the 2008 recession, target-date funds lost over 40 percent and the new Wall Street golden boy product was exposed. The only winner with target-funds was Wall Street! In 2008, Wall Street generated $2 billion in annual revenue from target-funds, and this has grown to over $13 billion in revenue in 2018.

The uncertainty of target-date funds is a scary thought if you've worked and saved diligently over twenty years. Many smart investors believed in the value of this product in early 2008, only to have the floor fall out from beneath them.

In our quest to build optimal investment strategies for ourselves, we'll need to take a hard look at how Wall Street charges us for their services. In the next chapter, we're going to discuss the common fee structures on Wall Street and alternative products and how these fees make building and preserving wealth more difficult. Don't worry, there is a solution; we just need to understand what's happening to our money before we can move forward!

---

8 "Testimony by Behavioral Research Associates Hearing on Target-Date Funds," Behavioral Research Associates, June 18, 2009.

KEY TAKEAWAYS

- → One in three Americans doesn't know what a financial advisor does. Do you know? Do you know how your advisor affects your investment portfolio?
- → The current state of the financial service industry is in desperate need of change.
- → The average rate of return of the S&P 500 between 1999 and 2018 was a mere 5.13 percent, but the actual return to the investor was only 3.82 percent and this is before expenses and fees.
- → Seventy-five percent of Americans can expect to see their assets disappear before they die, according to Ernst and Young.
- → The 401(k) was never intended to be a vehicle for retirement. The device doesn't guarantee returns, fees, income, or principal invested.
- → Warren Buffett, with his vast resources and experience, hasn't beaten the S&P 500 since 2008. Do you really think your trusted financial advisor selling annuities and mutual funds can do better?

CHAPTER 3

DEATH, TAXES AND WALL STREET FEES

"Fees never sleep."

—WARREN BUFFETT

Want to learn something astonishing? I'm going to show you how to make an easy $250,000 right now, with no effort on your part. Are you ready? It's all about fees or lack of fees!

Warren Buffett was once asked: how does Wall Street make so much money? He answered: "Fees never sleep." Not only do Wall Street fees never sleep—they're a thief in the night that will destroy your life savings.

Here's a simple example of three friends: Kim, David, and Tommy. All three friends invested $100,000 at the age of thirty-five. Each friend selected a different mutual fund and successfully have an equal return performance of 7 percent annually. At the age of sixty-five, all three friends get together at a 4th of July party and compare account balances. You've probably guessed where I'm going with this... All three friends received 7 percent annually in return, but they individually paid different fee structures in their mutual funds. Let's take a look at the effects:

- Kim invested $100,000 at 7 percent (minus 3 percent in annual fees), which equals an account balance of $324,340.
- David invested $100,000 at 7 percent (minus 2 percent in annual fees), which equals an account balance of $432,194.
- Tommy invested $100,000 at 7 percent (minus 1 percent in annual fees), which equals an account balance of $574,349.

That's a $250,000-dollar difference between Kim and Tommy.

If you're curious what hidden fees could be lurking within your investments, email me directly at mbrown@redfoxcommercialllc.com and our firm will provide a FREE analysis of what fees you're really paying and how it affects your future wealth.

But even minimal fees can be devastating. Let's take a look at real returns in the S&P 500 between January 1, 2000, and December 31, 2012. This period in time is referred to as the "lost decade" because the market was flat with no return but still had extreme volatility. If you invested $100,000 during the "lost decade" and realized flat returns with the minimal fee structure, what do you suppose happened? You lost money. If you paid the average mutual fund operating fee of 3.1 percent and your fund achieved the market return, you would have paid over $30,000 in fees. On top of that, your financial advisor charged you a 1 percent fee and made off with another $10,000 of your money. You invested the capital, took all the risk, and your account is down 40 percent with only $60,000 left because the market was flat. Guess what? The mutual fund made $30,000 and your financial advisor made $10,000 all without any risk. Think about it.

Now if we're paying these mutual fund managers top dollars in fees, shouldn't they be delivering above-average returns? Robert Arnott, the founder of Research Affiliates, studied mutual fund performance and can answer this question. Out of 203 actively managed mutual funds with at least $100 million in assets, 8 funds actually beat the S&P 500. That's less than 4 percent, with an astonishing 96 percent of these professional mutual fund managers being failures. I've always believed only weathermen and economists could stay employed with these stats.[9]

9 Vesna Poljak, "Robert Arnott on the Enemy of Successful Investing," *Financial Review*, November 18, 2018, https://www.afr.com/markets/equity-markets/rob-arnott-on-the-enemy-of-successful-investing-20181118-h180y3.

If that does not shock you, how about this: if you've ever played blackjack, the goal is to get as close to 21 without going bust. An article titled "Made to Stick: The Myth of Mutual Funds" states: "If you get dealt two face cards in blackjack (each face card is worth 10, so now your total is 20), and your inner idiot shouts, 'Hit me!' you have about an 8 percent chance of winning!"[10] That's *double* the 4 percent odds of beating the market with a professionally managed mutual fund!

Why does the status-quo financial advisor put your money in these high-fee Wall Street products? Because it makes the Wall Street machine and your financial advisor rich. A former JPMorgan Chase banker said to Reuters: "The consumer is simply an income stream and exploiting that is the purpose of the banking organization."[11] A year later, the *New York Times* published allegations that JPMorgan Chase advisors were forced by management to push their branded mutual funds on clients, even when better-performing funds with lower fees were available.[12]

Recently, I witnessed an advertisement by Edward Jones to recruit financial advisors. It told potential recruits:

10 "Made to Stick: The Myth of Mutual Funds," *Fast Company*, September 1, 2018.

11 Matthew Goldstein, Jennifer Ablan, "Insight: The Wall Street Disconnect," *Reuters*, November 18, 2011, https://www.reuters.com/article/us-wallst-disconnect/insight-the-wall-street-disconnect-idUSTRE7AH0Z620111118.

12 *New York Times*, December 4, 2015.

"Excelling here doesn't require a finance degree or a financial background. Successful graduates will experience unlimited earning potential with commissions based on your sales and incentive travel opportunities to places like Hawaii, Africa, Caribbean, China and more." Is this who you want to be in charge of your money? The federal government has made attempts to place higher fiduciary standards on financial institutions without much success. Senator Peter Fitzgerald cosponsored the Mutual Fund Reform Act of 2004, and it was quickly killed by the Wall Street lobby machine. The legislation never made it out of the Senate Banking Commission. Senator Fitzgerald said: "The mutual fund industry is now the world's largest skimming operation, a $7 trillion trough from which fund managers, brokers, and other insiders are steadily siphoning off an excessive slice of the nation's household, college, and retirement savings."

Nobody on Wall Street wants higher standards...

According to the *New York Times*, Morgan Stanley alone could lose $300 million in revenue if held to higher fiduciary standards.[13] Throughout my investing days and business endeavors, I've subscribed to full disclosure and full transparency. During the research of this book, I discovered to my disgust that Wall Street defines full disclosure and transparency in a different way.

13 *New York Times*, May 19, 2005.

FUN FACT

Warren Buffett still lives in the same house he purchased in 1958 for only $31,500.

Mutual funds and Wall Street products often refer to the expense ratio, load, or fee to explain the cost to owning the investment. One would think this was the fee, but it's only the beginning. Professor Robert Hiltonsmith, who has a PhD in economics, authored a report titled "The Retirement Savings Drain: The Hidden & Excessive Costs of 401(k)s."[14] The professor began researching Wall Street after noticing that his investment account would rarely rise in value no matter how the market was performing. He diligently read his fifty-page prospectus for each of the twenty funds he owned. He discovered that more than seventeen different fees were being charged in the fund, with another list of additional fees passed on to the investors.

Wall Street has become the expert at using complex terminology and legal structures to hide all the fees charged to investors. It is nearly impossible to make wealth with the current fee structures. In Professor Hiltonsmith's report, the average worker making $30,000 a year who invests 5 percent of his income into a retirement fund will

14 Jaime Catmull, "Do You Know How Much 401(k) Fees Are Costing You?," Forbes, December 8, 2018, https://www.forbes.com/sites/jaimecatmull/2018/12/08/do-you-know-how-much-401k-fees-are-costing-you/#59043637569c.

lose $154,794 in fees over his lifetime. A worker making $90,000 a year investing 5 percent of his income annually will lose $277,000 in fees. It's hard enough when 96 percent of fund managers can't beat the market, but with excessive fees passed along to investors, it's damn near impossible to build and preserve wealth.

3.1 TYPES OF MUTUAL FUND FEES

Now, not all fees are bad. People need to make a living for their knowledge and efforts. The key point being made is about *excessive* fees and knowing what they are. If you can lower your overall total annual fee structure to 1.25 percent or less, your financial health will dramatically increase. The key is understanding fees and recognizing when you're being exploited. It's important for investors to know what to look for when analyzing investments. Let's summarize the most common mutual fund fees and how they impact your investments.

- Expense ratio: Otherwise known as the total annual fund operating expenses. This fee tells the investor what percentage of the fund's total assets goes toward paying its fees every year.
- Management fees: These fees are paid to the investment advisor who runs the fund. These fees are accrued daily and usually paid monthly or quarterly.
- 12b-1 fees: These fees are capped at 1 percent of your

assets in the fund annually and taken out of the fund's assets to pay for the cost of marketing and selling the fund.

- Other expenses: These fees include costs of providing services to shareholders outside of the expenses covered by 12b-1 fees or portfolio management fees. The investor also pays transaction fees for the trades the fund makes; this amount is not reported separately as the other fees are.
- Account fees: Funds may charge you a separate fee to maintain your account. This commonly occurs when your investment falls below an established dollar amount.
- Redemption fees: These fees are charged when the investor sells or exchanges a fund. The fees discourage short-term trading and are charged to investors who sell their shares shortly after purchasing. Redemption fees may be charged anywhere from a few days to over a year.
- Exchange fees: Some funds charge exchange fees for moving your money from one fund to another fund offered by the same investment company.
- Purchase fees: Even if a fund decides not to charge a front-end sales charge, it may assess a purchase fee at the time the investor buys shares of the fund.
- Sales charge known as load: This fee is paid as a commission to the broker. These fees are NOT included in the expense ratio.

3.2. FEES FOR ALTERNATIVE INVESTMENTS

Wall Street and mutual funds are not exclusive in the area of fees. The other side of the investment world—most notably, real estate—can also be fee burdened. I've made a list of common fees associated with real estate investment funds. Again, it's important for investors to understand and know how to analyze these investment vehicles before they invest.

- Real estate brokerage fees: This fee compensates the broker that handles the search and disposition of real estate assets within a fund.
- Loan brokerage fees: These fees are associated with the loan broker identifying the proper debt mechanism and the management of the loan process.
- Capital raising fees: Capital raising consultants are common participants in real estate funds and can participate in many ways. One way is to earn a commission between 3 percent and 10 percent of the capital raised or to participate in equity within the fund.
- Acquisition fees: Some real estate funds charge an acquisition fee for the act of acquiring the property in addition to third-party brokerage fees.
- Organization fees: Real estate funds charge fees for putting the fund together. This is typically a percentage of the deal. For example, 1 or 2 percent of the total assets acquired might be charged.
- Leasing fees: Fees are charged for leasing space within

the particular asset. Professional assistance from a third-party real estate broker may also be used.

- Maintenance fees: Some real estate funds require maintenance departments to maintain properties. This can include landscape, painting, and other repair maintenance activities.
- Annual asset management fee: A real estate fund may earn an annual fee in managing the investor's assets.
- Development related fee: If a fund participates in real estate development activity, a development fee is charged for development, architectural, construction, and engineering services.
- Administrative fees: A fee for overseeing tax and accounting services for the investment.

3.3. CALCULATING AND COMPARING RETURNS

Are fees presented the same on Wall Street as they are in real estate? Not at all, and this is very tricky. To accurately analyze investment fees, it's important to compare Wall Street and alternative investments (such as real estate) as apples to apples.

Common practice among these asset classes is to present the returns and fees in different ways. Investors need to pay close attention. When your financial advisor says the S&P 500 has returned an average of 5.13 percent over the last twenty years, they don't explain how the annual average return is calculated over that time period. What they're failing to mention is the return is calculated *before* any fees are calculated. This simple exclusion dramatically distorts the annual average returns. Returns on real estate, on the other hand, usually speak about returns taking fees into account.

Not all fees are bad; they are necessary for investment professionals to earn a living and be compensated for their expertise and time. The important thing is to know what the fees are and how they are being measured against one another. Often investors think one investment has better overall returns, but in reality, it's not reality. Returns should not be interpreted the same across other asset classes. Returns are not created equal, and they should be analyzed as such.

For example, Preqin is the leader in tracking private investment performance, including real estate. Preqin presents the historical performance of real estate funds *after* fees, including commissions, carried interest, and the management fees paid to the fund managers. The key point is that the returns are calculated after all fees and expenses. This means that if a fund has an internal rate of return (IRR) of 15 percent, that's the investor's actual return while the investor participates in the investment.

When reviewing the historical performance on real estate assets, you will typically see the returns projected over the life of the investment. A few common calculations to compare investments are below:

- **Cash on cash:** The annual return the investor made of the property in relation to the amount of mortgage paid during the same year. In other words, it calculates the percentage of the initial investment that is returned to the investor each given time period (year) as the asset cash flows are collected.
- **Return on investment (ROI):** The calculation as a percentage of profit achieved by the investment over the total life of the investment. For example, a 100 percent ROI means you've doubled your investment.
- **Internal rate of return (IRR):** The internal rate of return for an investment is the percentage rate earned on each dollar invested for each time period it's invested. The IRR can also be seen as a discount rate that makes the net present value (NPV) of all cash flows from a particular project equal zero.

Let's use the IRR in an example. Say you're comparing two investments with the same return on investment (ROI), but one investment was held for five years and the other investment was only held for three years. This means the second investment held for three years would have a higher return due to the shorter time period.

Back to Wall Street and the S&P 500. If you analyze the IRR

MIKE'S LAW #3

Keep Expenses Low

Most investors have no idea how much they are paying in fees. Being aware and limiting your investment-related fees and expenses is critical. Simply reducing your expenses can dramatically increase your return on investment without any additional risk.

of the S&P 500 over the last twenty years and after fees, the overall return is only 2.74 percent. Financial advisors only speak of the overall average annual return of 5.13 percent. To accurately analyze the performance of the S&P 500 as compared to private commercial real estate, you must compare apples to apples with a 2.60 percent IRR over the last twenty years. Over those same twenty years, according to Prequin (a research and data firm), small private commercial real estate funds performed with an average IRR of 11.2 percent.

Later in the book, we're going to show you some exciting comparisons between the S&P 500 and private commercial real estate. This alone will unlock the secret to doubling your money in a straightforward strategy.

There is a significant difference between the way in which the stock market is measured when compared to private commercial real estate and other alternative investments. Just remember when comparing markets to alternative investments, markets show you average simple annual returns *before* fees, while alternatives show you a calculation that takes into account the time value of money and the compounding effect net of fees and any other expenses.

In the beginning of the book, we discussed the inherent conflicts of interest found on Wall Street and the financial service industry. In our journey to build a partnership of consensus among our financial advisors, we need to uncover what motivates their investment decision making. In the next chapter, we're going to learn how to challenge the status-quo financial advisor and discover how they're holding back on the best-known asset allocation strategy available to investors.

KEY TAKEAWAYS

→ Wall Street thrives on lowered standards, high fees, and selling branded proprietary products.

→ Mutual funds lead the way for high fees and are most common in today's retirement investment plans.

→ Out of 203 actively managed mutual funds with at least $100 million in assets, eight funds actually beat the S&P 500. That's less than 4 percent, with an astonishing 96 percent of these professional mutual fund managers being failures.

→ The wirehouse brokerage firms, like Merrill Lynch, UBS, and Morgan Stanley, alone each could lose over $300 million in revenue if held to higher fiduciary standards, according to the *New York Times*.

→ If you can lower your annual fee structure to 1.25 percent or less, your financial health will dramatically increase.

→ Over the last twenty years, the S&P has an internal rate of return (IRR) of 2.60 percent while small private commercial real estate funds have an IRR of 11.2 percent.

CHAPTER 4

WHY FINANCIAL ADVISORS IGNORE COMMERCIAL REAL ESTATE

"It is well enough that people of the nation do not understand our banking and monetary system. For if they did, I believe there would be a revolution before tomorrow morning."

—HENRY FORD

Are you crazy? Do you really want to be a landlord?

This is a popular response from financial advisors when presented with the idea of investing in real estate. Or they say that real estate is a wildly volatile market, or that real estate isn't liquid. Can you find a knowledgeable real estate agent you can trust? How could you possibly manage the day-to-day operations of your investment property?

Quick disclosure: Not all financial advisors have deceptive intentions when it comes to giving their clients investment advice. But isn't it true that more millionaires are created by real estate than any other means?

Andrew Carnegie, a billionaire industrialist, famously said: "Ninety percent of all millionaires become so through owning real estate. More money has been made in real estate than in all industrial investments combined. The wise young man or wage earner of today invests his money in real estate."

If someone like Andrew Carnegie believed in allocating real estate assets into investment portfolios, maybe we should consider such advice.

I've had the opportunity to review countless investment portfolios of wealthy clients. The simple success principle found in best-of-class portfolios was a proper allocation of private commercial real estate. Not only do I participate in the principle personally, but I find it necessary in all investment portfolios to counter the Wall Street markets and maintain an asset allocation that is counter-correlated.

Let's step back and take an in-depth look at exactly why financial advisors do not want you investing in real estate.

4.1. WHY ARE FINANCIAL ADVISORS AGAINST REAL ESTATE?

There are two answers to this question and they're both connected. The logical and most accurate answer is because the advisor will not earn fees or commissions if you invest in real estate. And the second answer is that they really don't understand the asset class and are embarrassed to admit it. I learned this to be true while working side by side with Merrill Lynch's most successful financial advisors. But is that in your best interest? Is that a responsible fiduciary approach from your financial advisor? Whether you like his politics or not, the president of the United States, Donald J. Trump, is a billionaire real estate investor, and he says: "Sometimes, your best investments are actually the ones you don't make." Could your financial advisor be holding back some of the best investments for your portfolio?

If any industry needs a disruption, it's the financial service industry. We need financial advisors in our lives, but we also need a better way to drive investment returns in a safer and more consistent way. But it's difficult to disrupt a mega powerful industry such as Wall Street. Most financial advisors don't have any knowledge or experience with real estate investments—and they don't have any incentive to acquire some. Most real estate investors and financial advisors don't have the opportunity or desire to spend the necessary time and energy to experience my unique perspective. Remember, I was a bit insane to undertake my wealth management training at the time.

Does this make sense from the perspective of an investor paying financial advisor fees? This becomes a natural conflict between investors and financial advisors. I began to see this with my colleagues in the financial advisor business; advisors only recommended company-sponsored investment products that were not always the best choice for the client. I can guarantee that most financial advisors have no idea what they're recommending to their clients. It became unbearable knowing what I knew from the commercial real estate world and what these financial advisors were doing to their clients. As discussed earlier in the book, financial advisors don't provide clients options beyond Wall Street, even though they may have their clients' best interests at heart; they just aren't trained properly on asset allocation principles. According to the Bankrate Financial Security Index Survey, more than fifty-four million Americans preferred to invest in real estate investments over stocks or bonds.[15] It's estimated that more than thirty million Americans are currently invested in both commercial and residential real estate investments. With this statistic, shouldn't financial advisors at least have a working knowledge of real estate investments?

From my experience, our wealthiest clients come into the office to review their stock portfolio on a regular basis. No matter how the stock markets are reacting, these clients

15 "You Probably Have the Wrong Idea When It Comes to Investments. Let's Fix That," Bankrate, July 19, 2017.

are always cool cucumbers and don't seem to have a worry in the world. On the other hand, other clients are worried about their 401(k) and stock portfolios every time they see the markets dip.

So I finally asked the question to those wealthy clients: "Why are you so relaxed with the stock market ups and downs?" Every time I asked, I heard the same answer: *My real estate portfolio provides my income cash flow. I never rely on Wall Street for my financial security.* This was a turning point in my life. How could I honestly provide investment advice without discussing real estate?

Now let's get real. The honest reason financial advisors, in general, do not want you investing in real estate is because their compensation plans do not allow it. It's not lucrative for advisors to recommend their clients go into real estate investments, because it doesn't provide big fees and commissions. Let's take a look at a few traditional compensation structures for financial advisors.

First, the "commission based" compensation structure. This advisor recommends traditional Wall Street products for their clients. When the client decides to add these products to their portfolio, the advisor receives a very handsome fee and commission. There are inherently many conflicts of interest in this structure. As an investor, you never really know if their advice benefits you or their bank account.

> **MIKE'S LAW #4**
>
> **Use Risk Management Strategies**
>
> If you're a sports fan, you know defense wins championships. Aggressive investing is fun when it works out, but smart investors realize that not losing money can be just as fun. Remember Warren Buffett's rules of investing:
>
> Rule #1: Don't lose money.
>
> Rule #2: Never forget rule #1.
>
> This doesn't mean an investor should not take risk—quite the contrary. It's just important not to lose principal, and one must implement risk management strategies that will hedge your downside. Investors need to prepare for stock market volatility that can be an investment return killer. Private commercial real estate is a favorite risk management technique due to the simple fact that your principal value will never revert to zero.

Second, the "assets under management" (AUM) compensation structure. This is most common among today's financial advisors. Basically, the advisor places all of your assets into a portfolio compiled of traditional Wall Street stocks and bonds and manages this portfolio in your interest. In return for their management efforts, the advisor charges you an average fee of about 1 percent. For example, if you have a portfolio of $1 million, the advisor would be compensated $10,000 a year.

In summary, a financial advisor working under the "commission based" structure would not recommend real estate investments for your investment strategy, because they will not receive any fees in return. Advisors never want assets leaving their control. The advisor working with AUM makes their fees from investments under management; real estate investments are not under their direct management and, therefore, there are no fees.

If you want to understand business, just understand the motivations behind the person you're dealing with, and always track the flow of money.

4.3. HOW WALL STREET INVESTS IN REAL ESTATE

Say you find a financial advisor that does offer private real estate investments. They make it a part of their financial strategy. You think: "Right, I've got this covered now." But that may not be the case. The value of investing in real estate is that it's an *alternative* investment—as different from Wall Street as you can get. And what most financial managers will recommend to you as "real estate" is not that.

Let me explain. Have you ever heard the phrase "No one ever got fired for hiring IBM"? Most financial advisors prefer to recommend multibillion-dollar real estate managers like Blackstone and Carlyle or other high-fee Real Estate Investment Trusts (REITs), rather than work with smaller managers who most likely can and will outperform these high-profile larger players. The issue with these alternative solutions is they are all correlated to Wall Street markets. REITs are nothing more than a common mutual fund compiled of real estate companies. But most financial advisors don't really understand this principle. REITs are openly traded on the stock market. REITs and some of these very large private real estate funds are the only real estate investment products available for the financial advisor community to sell. Therefore, the advisors get commissions! These REITs and large real estate private equity companies like Blackstone and Carlyle are not *alternative* in the true sense of the word.

This plan of attack is actually the worst thing an advisor can do and certainly is a great way to achieve average or below-average returns. Private real estate is not a business where high-fee products lead to better returns or where bigger is better. There is evidence that a strong inverse correlation exists between manager size and investment returns.

Historically, average private real estate managers investing less than $300 million outperform the top-tier multibillion-dollar managers like Blackstone. The performance is not marginal; smaller fund managers commonly outperform their multibillion-dollar managers by double. But the safe play is to revert to "No one ever got fired for hiring IBM," and so advisors recommend the big names to their investors because they are considered safe.

Companies like JPMorgan, Merrill Lynch, Goldman Sachs, and Morgan Stanley would never bring clients to smaller real estate managers because investing $50 million into a fund doesn't generate enough revenue for their businesses. These companies have billions of dollars to place and do not want to spend the time and energy to underwrite multiple smaller fund managers and syndications. So they settle for the large, well-known companies, such as Blackstone and Carlyle. By doing this, they deprive their clients of the opportunity to invest with smaller managers that are able to provide superior returns on investments.

Moreover, the smaller real estate funds cannot afford the very expensive underwriting criteria all large investment brokerages require. This should not disqualify a small fund—quite the opposite. It makes no sense to spend hundreds of thousands of dollars on wasteful due diligence when the money should be used to enhance investment returns for their investors.

In the next chapter, we'll delve more fully into the world of commercial real estate—these small funds that can help your returns flourish. Bringing private commercial real estate into your asset allocation is so important, we're going to move away from Wall Street and devote the next few chapters to understanding it in depth. Real estate investing is not exactly as you may think; there are many types, methods, and myths. I'm here to guide you through it.

KEY TAKEAWAYS

- → If any industry needs a disruption, it's the financial service industry. We need financial advisors in our lives, but we also need a better way to drive investment returns in a safer and more consistent way.
- → The honest reason financial advisors do not want you investing in private commercial real estate is because their commission plans do not allow it.
- → Smaller private real estate funds crush the larger billion-dollar private real estate funds by doubling the returns to their investors.

CHAPTER 5

PRIVATE COMMERCIAL REAL ESTATE AS AN ALTERNATIVE TO WALL STREET

"It ain't what you don't know that gets you in trouble. It's what you know for sure that just ain't so."

—MARK TWAIN

We've discussed how asset allocation is the most important decision an investor can make. We've also learned how true diversification does not mean a mutual fund or index fund, but a distribution of investments across many asset classes. Private commercial real estate is the best asset class to achieve the highest returns through the practice of asset allocation. Let's leave Wall Street for Main Street for the next few chapters.

FUN FACT

The famous Las Vegas strip is not located in the city of Las Vegas. To avoid taxes, the Strip is located in a city named Paradise.

Real estate investing is not all about flipping houses! The first thing an average investor thinks when confronted with real estate investing is residential homes, such as flipping or holding residential houses for rental cash flow. Today is the day I open a new world of real estate investing to you. This will dramatically impact your investment strategy, and open the door to a disruption in the financial service industry.

Commercial real estate—also referred to as private real estate and small private real estate funds in this book—is an important part of a diversified and properly allocated investment portfolio. However, it's still a complicated and confusing asset class for many investors. We're going to fix that problem.

First, let's define what private commercial real estate is and how it can benefit investors.

5.1. WHAT IS PRIVATE COMMERCIAL REAL ESTATE?

A private commercial real estate investment is any non-institutional grade and sized investment in one or more real estate based strategy. By definition, this would exclude the common institutional investments such as large hedge funds, REITs, pension funds, large private equity funds, banks, and other market participants that play in the large institutional space rather than the entrepreneurial space. So the polar opposite of private commercial real estate would be the large institutional real estate funds like Blackstone, Carlyle, and Starwood.

Average investment size for a private commercial real estate fund would fall between $2 million and $5 million. It's even possible to find solid deals as low as $1 million or less. A private commercial real estate fund is a structure that raises money and buys multiple properties within a fund. The total assets under management in these funds will fall around $100 million the majority of the time. But there are also excellent funds that operate in the $5 million to $50 million range.

In the United States today, there is more than $60 billion in private commercial real estate sales transactions annually (as a best estimate). This doesn't include any single-family residential investment property, private- or hard-money lending, distressed or discounted real estate notes, or any other investment strategy involving real estate as an asset class.

Let's break out a quick comparison between private commercial real estate and institutional real estate investments:

SMALL PRIVATE COMMERCIAL REAL ESTATE	INSTITUTIONAL REAL ESTATE
Deal size < $5M	Deal size >$25M or more
Institutional capital not available	Fund sizes >$500M or more
Highly fragmented	Small number of large players
Wide variety of strategies	Compressed yields
Fund size <$50M	Outdated strategies
High yields	Scalability required
Customized fund structures	Economic/terms rigid

The private commercial real estate industry is a huge market collectively; it is also highly fragmented and highly regionalized, even localized, which offers great opportunity. The institutional real estate players, such as Blackstone and Starwood, get all the media attention because it's an easier narrative. (It's also what your financial advisor will sell to you, as we explored in section 4.3 in the last chapter.) The private commercial real estate world, on the other hand, operates like a parallel universe to the institutional world, with little to no media attention. This is a good thing!

"I have a way of making money that you know nothing of."

—JOHN D. ROCKEFELLER

5.2. TYPES OF INVESTORS IN PRIVATE COMMERCIAL REAL ESTATE

What types of investors does private commercial real estate attract?

5.2.1. ACCREDITED HIGH-NET-WORTH INVESTORS

The most common investors taking advantage of private commercial real estate are accredited high-net-worth investors. The Securities Exchange Commission defines an accredited investor as someone with a net worth of at least $1 million, excluding the value of one's personal primary residence, or someone having an income of at least $200,000 each of the past two years or $300,000 combined with a spouse if married. It is estimated that around 3–4 percent of American households meet the accredited investor classification.

The majority of accredited investors in private commercial real estate have a net worth between $1 million and $10 million. This investment class will typically invest anywhere between $50,000 to $250,000 in each investment. It should be noted, however, that some private real estate investment companies have minimum and maximum investment levels.

5.2.2. ULTRA-HIGH-NET-WORTH INVESTORS

These investors are also classified as accredited, but have a much larger net worth and typically will invest a larger portion of their investment portfolio into private commercial real estate. Ultra-high-net-worth investors are in the top 1 percent of American households with net worths ranging from $10 million to over $50 million. Often, these investors are entrepreneurs or successful executives, and their mindsets are aligned with private real estate managers: they are looking to invest wisely so that they can slow their working intensity and rely on strong returns from their investments.

5.2.3. FAMILY OFFICES

Family offices are private companies that manage investments and trusts for wealthy families. Both single-family offices, which manage one family, or multifamily offices, which serve multiple wealthy families, participate in private commercial real estate. The average size of a family office is $800 million under management.[16] Professional wealth managers drive the investment strategy for the offices and rely on commercial real estate to obtain the performance expected from their clients.

Investors come in all shapes and sizes. One of my most unexpected investors came in the form of a small-statured man whom most would have overlooked. He wore overalls with his name embroidered on his chest and tracked a trail of mud into my office. I didn't know what to expect: was he here to talk about his investments?

The gentleman owned a successful asphalt company and was easily within the ultra-high-net-worth category. That brief introduction turned into many years of successful

16 Global Family Office Report 2018, CampdenWealth, September 25, 2018.

investing together. This gentleman had a knack for making money and considered the dirt beneath his real estate to be his brown gold. The lesson learned from this client was to always look at life from a different perspective, and that's where you'll find the value.

We just described the top 4 percent of wealthy households in the United States. Private commercial real estate has become a foundation pillar in their investment strategy. Why? Let's find out.

5.3. BENEFITS OF INCLUDING COMMERCIAL REAL ESTATE IN YOUR INVESTMENT STRATEGY

Investing in commercial real estate can be in the form of land, office buildings, apartments, shopping centers, hotels, industrial warehouses, self-storage, and more. This type of investing offers many benefits to individual investors, such as higher returns, portfolio diversification, tax efficiency, and noncorrelation to Wall Street.

Institutional investors have used commercial real estate in their portfolios to balance Wall Street uncertainty for generations. Yale University's endowment fund is considered the gold standard by most experts for its superb performance. Yale attributes its success to private commercial real estate; $27 billion to steward is a monumental responsibility, so take notice. Yale's endowment allocates 10 percent of its portfolio to commercial real estate. Other endowments and pension funds have taken notice and follow similar investment strategies.

Over the last few years, individual investors "in the know" are adding these investments to their portfolios with great success. Tiger 21, which is an exclusive peer-to-peer learning network for high-net-worth investors, whose members are required to have a minimum of $10 million in investable assets, consistently allocates between 25 percent and 30 percent of their investments to real estate.

Is it time you do the same?

MIKE'S LAW #5

Buy Cash Flow

Investing in assets with immediate cash flow gives investors return no matter how the investment performs in the long term. Don't bet on the investment's appreciation or better management. Cash flow hedges against problems that may arise in the future.

Identifying assets with strong fundamentals for tenant demand and high yield gives investors actual profits that can be reinvested or realized as a revenue income stream.

Combining cash flow as a primary factor in choosing your investment allocation along with appreciation will provide investors the best hedge for overall portfolio performance.

5.3.1. BENEFIT #1–COMMERCIAL REAL ESTATE GENERATES HIGH ABSOLUTE RETURNS

Commercial real estate provides the ability for investors to achieve higher absolute returns. An absolute higher return takes into consideration account appreciation, depreciation, and cash flows to demonstrate the amount of money an investment earns over time; it is expressed in terms of percentage gained or lost on the initial investment.

According to Prequin, a research company that tracks data for alternative investments, a $100,000 investment in the average commercial real estate fund beginning January 1, 2001, would have been worth about $380,000 on January 1, 2019. That same $100,000 investment in the S&P 500 would have been worth $167,162 on January 1, 2019.

5.3.2. BENEFIT #2—COMMERCIAL REAL ESTATE DOESN'T CORRELATE TO OTHER ASSET CLASSES

Most investors are satisfied with a diversified portfolio of stocks and bonds until Wall Street starts to get crazy with ups and downs. But, to be fair, most investors are never introduced to other alternative investments because our financial advisors don't provide them to clients. Commercial real estate, with its low correlation to Wall Street, helps investors temper the volatility in their portfolios because it's immune to the daily shocks of trading.

Every investment portfolio's goal should be to create the highest return with the least amount of volatility. The value of a commercial real estate asset is based on the actual value of the property. On the other hand, in a publicly traded REIT, the share price value is determined by daily market forces. This means that Wall Street determines the actual value of your asset and not the underlying real estate. Just think about this. Would you allow Wall Street to control the value of your home? It's possible for the value of a REIT to fluctuate 30 percent higher or lower than the actual value of the underlying real estate asset.

Commercial real estate appreciates slowly over time, which is why these assets are less volatile than Wall Street investment options. Commercial real estate has minimal correlation to stocks, bonds, and public REITs. The chart below by the National Council of Real Estate Investment Fiduciaries (NCREIF) property index (NPI), which measures the returns of private commercial real estate properties, demonstrates the low correlation with stock markets.[17]

Keep in mind, a correlation coefficient of zero (0) means that the price fluctuations are not correlated at all. A correlation coefficient of one (1) means the assets move together in tandem. A negative correlation means they move in opposite directions to one another. An investment

17 NCREIF.org.

portfolio benefits when it includes asset classes that are not correlated to each other.

NATIONAL COUNCIL OF REAL ESTATE INVESTMENT FIDUCIARIES

	RUSSELL 3000	BARCLAYS U.S. AGGREGATE	NAREIT
NCREIF	0.23	-0.24	0.13

Source: TIAA-CREF Asset Management[18]

5.3.3. BENEFIT #3—COMMERCIAL REAL ESTATE TAX EFFICIENCY

Many investors focus entirely on the returns and completely ignore the after-tax yields. This is a magical benefit to investing in commercial real estate. Income generated by real estate is shielded by the depreciation of the asset, which provides investors with the long-term benefits of substantial cash flow and a very small tax burden.

Since real estate assets will likely require capital expenditures as they age, such as a new HVAC system or paving the parking lot, the IRS allows investors to take annual losses in the form of depreciation to smoothen out these eventual capital expenditures. However, only the physical elements of the property may be depreciated; land cannot be depreciated.

Let's look at an example. An office building property can be

18 NCREIF.org.

straight-line depreciated over thirty-nine years. If the property was purchased for $6 million and the land is worth $1 million, it will produce $128,205 in annual noncash depreciation. This is calculated by dividing $5 million by 39 to yield $128,205 in depreciation dollars.

Most individuals pay between 20 percent and 25 percent in taxes on real estate investments versus the highest tax bracket of 37 percent on ordinary income, hedge funds, and other alternative investments. So if the real estate generates $100,000 of cash flow and $50,000 in depreciation, the taxable income to the individual investor will only be $50,000. The tax liability, assuming the investor is in the highest federal tax bracket, is calculated by 0.37 x $50,000 to yield $18,500, which is equivalent of an 18.5 percent tax rate on the entire cash flow of $100,000 dollars. This is one of the reasons why Warren Buffett famously pays a lower tax rate than his secretary.

The depreciated portion of the real estate is subject to a recapture rate of 25 percent upon sale. Here's how it works: if the real estate is purchased for $10 million and depreciated by $2 million, the cost basis for tax purposes would only be $8 million. This difference between the cost basis and the original purchase price is taxed at the recapture rate at the time of sale.

In addition, all real estate investment's appreciation above the original purchase price is subject to a 20 percent capital gains tax if the property is held for more than one year. Using our example, if the real estate was sold for $13 million, the difference of $2 million from the IRS tax basis of $8 million to the purchase basis of $10 million would be subject to the recapture rate of 25 percent. The gain from $10 million to $13 million would be taxed at the capital gains rate of 20 percent. Then, the effective overall tax liability at sale would be $500,000 + $600,000 or $1.1 million.

You've probably heard of another popular IRS tax benefit of real estate: the 1031 exchange. The 1031 exchange allows investors to defer taxes indefinitely. Investors are allowed to sell a like property and buy another like property without incurring capital gains tax. So, in theory, an investor could buy and sell real estate without ever paying capital gains taxes. The 1031 exchange was created in the spirit that all sales proceeds from the sale of the real estate would be reinvested in another asset. It would be unfair to tax cash proceeds never received by the investor. The 1031 exchange is one of the greatest benefits to investing in real estate and is employed every day in this country.

5.3.4. BENEFIT #4—THE POWER OF LEVERAGE

Let's first define "leverage." In the general sense of the word, leverage is any technique to multiply gains and losses. Leverage is simply borrowing money alongside equity to acquire real estate, and it greatly enhances your overall returns. Just like buying your home, not many buyers pay all cash, but take out mortgages that increase their buying power, a.k.a. leverage. By applying the power of leverage, you can achieve a lot more. Without the power of leverage, your rewards are restricted to only the amount of work or energy you put into a task.

To build and maintain wealth, it's absolutely necessary to employ the concept of leverage. On Wall Street, leverage is used in options, future contracts, and buying on margin to use borrowed stock shares from your broker to increase your position size so you can potentially make more money. It's a risky game, and I know plenty of people on the losing side of Wall Street leverage. The problem with using leverage on Wall Street is that you can lose much more money than originally invested. On the other hand, real estate cannot lose all its value; it's impossible. Once, we consulted with a high-net-worth client who learned the lesson of leverage the hard way. I'll never forget driving in the car with him as he frantically called his financial advisor demanding more leverage. Over a very short period, he had lost his entire $100 million net worth due to aggressively employing margin calls with his financial advisor. His investment was in an energy stock that had great and future promise. As the stock value spiraled down, he was faced with margin calls where he had to come up with sometimes $2 million in cash over a weekend to cover the stock losses.

Ultimately, the energy stock went to zero and the company faced bankruptcy protection.

On the other hand, using leverage with real estate is a safe and smart way to increase your investment returns. The underlying asset can never go to zero, as we just witnessed in the energy stock example. Real estate is a hard real asset and is impossible to drop to a zero valuation.

Using debt, whether from a bank, life insurance company, or pension fund, is much cheaper than equity. Commercial real estate has very efficient and well-established markets to obtain debt. This allows for the real estate borrower to negotiate the best terms for each individual asset through multiple sources.

In today's debt market on investment grade commercial real estate, common interest rates of around 5 percent or lower for debt are easy to achieve. Not only is the cost of the debt cheap; the lenders will also provide leverage up to 75 percent to 80 percent of the total asset cost, meaning the investor only needs to provide 20 percent to 25 percent of equity to purchase a property.

Let's look at an example of leverage:

	85 PERCENT LEVERAGE	70 PERCENT LEVERAGE
Cost	$20,000,000	$20,000,000
Equity	$3,000,000	$6,000,000
Debt	$17,000,000	$14,000,000
Sell amount	$25,000,000	$25,000,000
ACCRUED INTEREST		
At 4 percent over 2 year hold (*(ignoring amortization)*	$1,360,000	$1,120,000
Gain/Loss on investment	**$3,640,000**	**$3,880,000**
Total Return on Equity	**121 percent**	**65 percent**

Some will warn investors of the danger of leverage, but in commercial real estate it's actually a very low-risk proposition. Banks or any other provider of debt will only loan after a comprehensive appraisal is completed. The appraisal ensures the correct real estate valuation; then, and only then, will the debt provider loan a percentage of the total asset.

This concept allows for significant market collapse before any debt would ever be higher than the real estate asset's valuation. Most of today's commercial real estate debt mortgages have five- to ten-year term lengths, which gives the investor significant time to allow for market fluctuations in the event of a market recession or price regression. During the Great Recession, commercial real estate values were hit just like the residential real estate world, but recovered strongly within three to five years. With longer loan term lengths, real estate has the luxury of time to recover, unlike a risky margin call with a Wall Street stock.

More importantly, real estate loans typically cannot be called due to fluctuations in the market in the way leveraging stocks on margin can. If the stock price falls, the investor needs to make up the difference with cash on demand!

5.3.5 BENEFIT #5—ASSET-BASED COLLATERAL VS. WALL STREET

Commercial real estate assets are much more stable than your traditional Wall Street investments. When an investor purchases a real estate asset, you actually own the cash flow and the underlying asset that can be visited, seen, and touched.

During the Great Recession in 2008, commercial property values dropped by around 30 percent. Rental rates fell, property valuations dropped, and sales volume slowed considerably from $460 billion in 2007 to $70 billion in 2009 according to Real Estate Analytics.[19] This was no doubt the most difficult time in my life, but looking back, the education I received from the School of Hard Knocks proved better than any fancy Harvard MBA.

The main concern during the Great Recession besides property devaluation was the severe slowdown of deal velocity

19 NREIONLINE.com, October 28, 2019.

in the market. Real estate assets were not being sold or bought. During this time period, commercial real estate became very illiquid, and if an investor was in desperate need of equity, it was a problem. But most notably during this horrific real estate crash, the asset valuation never fell to zero. Can Wall Street say the same? I think not.

Within a couple of years following the Great Recession, most real estate had rebounded to prerecession prices and continue to appreciate. While the downturn certainly caused a lot of issues over the long term, it was not a catastrophic event for investors who could weather the storm.

The other unusual aspect we witnessed during the recession was the banks' uncanny desire to "extend and pretend" maturing commercial real estate loans. This is a cornerstone to the benefit of asset-based collateral. The banks knew these real estate assets would rebound and preferred to extend the current maturity date as long as the investors could continue to pay the debt service or even partially pay the mortgage. This would never occur with margin calls in the stock market.

Unlike commercial real estate over the last twenty years, we have witnessed the collapse of Wall Street darlings such as:

- **Enron**: At Enron's peak, its shares were worth $90.75 and had a market cap of $60 billion; when the company declared bankruptcy on December 2, 2001, the stock was trading at $0.26 a share. This complete collapse happened in less than twelve months.

- **WorldCom:** WorldCom was a $175 billion company at its peak, and its stock was trading above $60 a share in 2000. By the time the company declared bankruptcy in 2002, the stock was trading for as low as $.09 cents a share.
- **Sears:** Even the iconic American company Sears isn't immune to volatile markets. Sears' stock price dropped from over $40 a share in mid-2015 to under $0.90 in 2019.

This is a clear example of why having real estate as the underlying asset is a strong benefit, and why you should consider it when looking at your investment strategy.

5.3.6. BENEFIT #6—WHY NOT BEING LIQUID IS A GOOD THING

The liquidity issue with real estate investing is always considered one of the downsides. This is one of our friendly financial advisor's favorite kill shots to real estate. But can this issue with liquidity actually benefit investors?

A great book written by Gary Belsky and Thomas Gilovich called *Why Smart People Make Big Money Mistakes* addresses the issue of liquidity.[20] The authors asked the reader:

20 Gary Belsky and Thomas Gilovich, *Why Smart People Make Big Money Mistakes* (New York: Fireside, 2000), Behavioraleconomics.com.

> Imagine you have just been given $1,000 and have been asked to choose between two options. With option A, you are guaranteed to win an additional $500. With option B, you are given the chance to flip a coin. If it's heads, you receive another $1,000; tails, you get nothing more. Which option would you choose?
>
> Now imagine that you have just been given $2,000 and are required to choose between two options. With option A, you are guaranteed to lose $500. With option B, you are given the chance to flip a coin. If it's heads, you lose $1,000; tails, you lose nothing. Now which option would you choose?

This test illustrates why illiquidity can be a good thing. Studies have found that most people choose option A in the first example, the guaranteed $500 win, and option B in the second example. They take a chance to avoid the sure $500 loss. In other words, the human brain is wired to take on additional risk to avoid losses. When winning is a sure thing, the human brain prefers to act more conservatively. The authors describe this at an emotional level: "People feel more strongly about the pain that comes with a loss than they do about the pleasure that comes with an equal gain. These examples demonstrate why people make stupid decisions."

When investing, a common stupid mistake is panic selling. The pain of a stock market crash is so great, investors sell at the bottom. Nejat Seyhun, another researcher, says: "By putting your money out in short-term drops, you run the risk of missing those productive days. And it's serious risk... If you missed the 90 best performing days of the stock market from 1963 to 2004, your average annual return would have dropped from almost 11 percent return, assuming you had stayed fully invested, to slightly more than 3 percent... On a $1,000 investment, those different rates of return translate into the difference between having $74,000 after four decades or having $3,200."[21]

This scenario just can't happen in commercial real estate investing. Impulsive decisions are insulated by the slow and steady processes in real estate. An investor cannot wake up on Monday morning and sell a $5 million shopping center by noon. Numerous studies prove anywhere up to 50 percent of investors check their stock portfolios once a week if not more. This can be a costly habit and probably not good for one's blood pressure.

Commercial real estate comes in all sizes and shapes. In the next chapter, we're going to explain the many types of real estate assets and the pros and cons for each type. We'll learn what type of commercial real estate fits your investment style and goals best.

21 Carole Gould, "Five Portfolios Lose but Hold to Course," *New York Times*, January 7, 1995, https://www.nytimes.com/1995/01/07/business/five-portfolios-lose-but-hold-to-course.html.

KEY TAKEAWAYS

- → Diversification isn't about investing in one hundred stocks and hoping for the best; true diversification is best achieved when investing across several asset classes, such as equities, bonds, real estate, and private equity with a low correlation to each other.
- → Commercial real estate—also referred to as private real estate and small private real estate funds—is an important part of a diversified and properly allocated investment portfolio.
- → The private commercial real estate industry is a huge market collectively; it is also highly fragmented and highly regionalized, even localized, which brings great opportunity.
- → Commercial real estate has minimal correlation to stocks, bonds, and public REITs.
- → There are tax efficiencies for individuals investing in commercial real estate. Investors pay between 20 percent and 25 percent in taxes on these investments, versus the 37 percent on ordinary income, hedge funds, and other alternative investments.
- → The wealthy investor allocates 25–30 percent of their assets into real estate.

CHAPTER 6

ASSORTMENT OF ASSET CLASSES IN COMMERCIAL REAL ESTATE

"God loves diversity. He doesn't want everything exactly alike."

—RICK WARREN

Most people think commercial real estate investing is only about leasing office buildings. But commercial real estate actually offers many diverse asset classes that you can invest in, and these have different potential impacts on your investment portfolio. In this chapter, we'll give a detailed overview on each asset class so you'll feel more comfortable with commercial real estate investing. Then we'll discuss how you should combine asset classes to make the most of your investments.

FUN FACT

When Apple was building a new data server in North Carolina, they paid one elderly couple $1.7 million for one acre of land. The couple had originally purchased the property thirty-four years earlier for $6,000.

6.1. TYPES OF COMMERCIAL REAL ESTATE

The world of commercial real estate is generally divided into four asset classes: office, industrial, retail, and multifamily. Each of these asset classes can be further divided into subcategories. For example, there are numerous types of industrial properties. Moreover, beyond the main four asset classes, other property types exist, such as hotels, self-storage, medical offices, senior housing, land, and others.

Finally, each asset class can be labeled by quality, such as Class A, B, or C. Each asset class is analyzed differently and requires different information to make an informed investment decision.

6.1.1 OFFICE

Office buildings can come in many different sizes, from a New York City skyscraper to a one-story brick building in Anytown, USA. The US office market attracts a large amount of investment capital from both institutional and private investors.

The National Council of Real Estate Investment Fiduciaries (NCREIF) Index shows a healthy return of 10.3 percent over the past twenty years for office building investments.[22] One reason why office building investment is popular is due to the strong underlying fundamentals, a diverse base of users that span from technology companies to professional services. Let's take an overview look at the office asset class, and how investors can use this information when making investment decisions.

Office buildings are usually classified into two categories based on where they are located: (1) the central business district (CBD) and (2) anything not in the CBD, referred to as the suburban area. The asset can also be categorized by a property grade of Class A, B, or C, based on criteria such as age, quality, amenities, size, rent, and location.

The CBD is the downtown concentration of office use in any main city or town. On the other hand, suburban offices are located in lower-density areas outside of the urban core. Office tenants attracted to the CBD tend to be more established professional companies, while smaller and emerging groups are attracted to the relatively lower costs of being in the suburbs.

Office buildings also vary by use. The most common is general office use, with primarily professional service ten-

22 NCREIF.com

ants. General office buildings have few specialized tenant improvements and, therefore, make it cheaper for tenant rollover, unlike medical offices that require significant tenant improvements specific to medical use and can be more difficult to convert to another tenant in the event of tenant rollover.

The Building Owners and Managers Association (BOMA) distinguishes office buildings by the number of floors.[23]

- Low rise: Fewer than seven stories above the ground
- Mid rise: Between seven and twenty-five stories above the ground
- High rise: More than twenty-five stories above the ground

Building size by floor classification will impact the type of tenants the office building attracts. High-rise buildings may attract top-tier law firms to impress clients and entice top employees. A creative company such as a digital marketing agency may prefer a low-rise with easy access and more relaxed rules, such as bringing your dog to work and free parking.

It's important for office investors to understand what drives value in this asset class. Strong employment correlates to positive office valuations; jobs demand more office space

23 "BOMA Floor Measurement Standards," BOMA.org.

as companies hire new employees. Moreover, studying how demographics affect office demand can give investors insights into how the asset class might perform. Millennials will soon represent the largest segment of workers. Landlords are positioning their buildings toward millennial preferences. Walk into any WeWork space, and you'll know exactly what I'm describing. These office spaces look more like cool living spaces versus the past days of office cubicles. In addition, these workers demand amenities such as coffee bars, gyms, yoga classes, etc. Having a basic understanding of demographics will factor into new building design and use, and it becomes easier to contemplate the alternative workplace strategies that are changing how and where people chose to work.

With the mass adoption of mobile technology, some believe that traditional office buildings may soon become dinosaurs. A more pragmatic approach suggests that the way in which office space is used is changing, but there is still demand. Working at home or the local coffee shop is not effective for everyone or every business. Office buildings are not going anywhere in the future.

6.1.2. INDUSTRIAL

Industrial buildings are used for functions such as manufacturing, research and development, storage, and distribution of goods. Because these properties require a lot of acreage for wide building footprints, low-density parking, and truck turning, they are almost never found in the CBD. The three main categories of industrial buildings are manufacturing, warehouse, and flex/R&D. These categories are defined by the National Association of Industrial and Office Parks as follows:[24]

- **Manufacturing**: This refers to a facility used for the conversion, fabrication, and/or assembly of raw or partly wrought materials into products/goods. These properties tend to have less than 20 percent office space and can be further classified for a heavy or light industrial use.
- **Warehouse**: This is a facility primarily used for the storage and/or distribution of materials, goods, and merchandise. These buildings tend to have less than 15 percent office space, and modern facilities have high clear ceiling heights that allow for more cubic storage space. This category also may include specialty facilities, such as cold or freezer storage for food.
- **Flex/R&D**: These industrial buildings are designed to give their occupants flexibility regarding the use of space. Sometimes referred to as flex/tech space, these buildings are an office-industrial hybrid that can have 30 percent to even 100 percent office finish.

The industrial asset class is often seen as the least glamor-

24 NAIOP.org.

ous of the commercial real estate classes. Don't be fooled: these properties are steady investment performers. The average annual return for industrial properties over the past twenty years is 10.6 percent. Factors to consider when looking at industrial properties are location, proximity to customers and employees, transportation, access to land, and financial incentives that can offset building expenses.

One phenomenon that is driving huge demand for industrial properties is the growth of e-commerce. According to CoStar, since 2010, one-third of all industrial leases over 500,000 square feet are being leased by e-commerce users.[25] Forrester Research projects that US e-commerce sales will surpass $400 billion by 2019.[26] This demand makes industrial real estate a great asset class for any investment portfolio.

6.1.3. RETAIL

Despite the perception that e-commerce is going to destroy brick-and-mortar retail, the retail asset class has a track record of solid returns. We often refer to certain retail as "Amazon proof," such as nail salons, dry cleaning, family restaurants, barbershops, and even medical uses. Never underestimate the power of Amazon, but these retail uses are likely off the radar for Amazon, at least for now.

25 Crowdstreet, August 12, 2016.

26 Digitalcommerce360.com, April 2, 2015.

Recently, retail demand is high, with historically aggressive cap rates as low as 3 percent. Vacancy rates have also remained low, even with the competition of e-commerce.

Retail properties can range from a single tenant building such as a Walgreens to large mega shopping malls. The International Council of Shopping Centers (ICSC), the largest retail industry organization in the world, defines the various retail classes as follows:[27]

- **Malls:** Regional malls range in size from about 400,000 to 800,000 square feet and include inline retail, service and restaurant tenants, as well as major department store anchors, such as Macy's and Nordstrom. Super-regional malls are upward of 800,000 square feet.
- **Community and Neighborhood Centers:** These centers are "anchored" by a big-box retailer such as Target, Walmart, or a grocery store. These centers might range in size from 30,000 to 400,000 square feet.
- **Strip Centers:** Named for their straight configuration, these centers generally focus on convenience tenants such as dry cleaners, nail salons, and sandwich shops. Strip centers are smaller than 30,000 square feet.
- **Power Centers:** These centers are dominated by big-box retailers such as Best Buy, Dick's Sporting Goods, and Bed Bath & Beyond with only a few small tenants.
- **Lifestyle Centers:** As enclosed malls become too

27 ICSC.com.

expensive to build, it created a new generation of open-air lifestyle centers that feature upscale apparel and other retailers, along with dining and entertainment.

Retail has historically commanded the highest price per square foot than any other real estate asset class. In 2014, Chanel in New York City broke a record by paying $31,000 a square foot. On average, retail has produced average annual returns of 10.8 percent over the past twenty years, according to data from the National Council of Real Estate Investment Fiduciaries (NCREIF) Index.[28]

An important value driver for retail is its dependency on traffic and parking. Urban retail spaces, which usually are a portion of a mixed-use building rather than a single-use building, rely heavily upon foot traffic, while strip centers rely heavily on vehicle traffic. Lifestyle centers, on the other hand, will create their own traffic because the anchor tenants are usually destination tenants, such as movie theaters and restaurants. Except for the densest urban locations, almost all retail tenants require minimum parking to square footage ratios in order to lease space.

Another important feature of retail property is the tenant mix. While multifamily and office tenants usually do not care who their neighbors are as long as they are quiet, retail tenants thrive off certain neighbors and refuse to be located

28 NCREIF.org

near others, usually competitors. For example, you may find a Jo-Ann Fabrics located in the same shopping center as a Big Lots or Dollar Tree. This strategy is referred to as adjacencies. Having appropriate tenant mix is something of an art in retail real estate.

When looking at a retail asset, think about what kind of customer experience the real estate is currently providing or what kind of experience it could provide in the hands of the right operator. If you can't envision a good experience in any scenario, it's safest to stay away. However, if you see a great experience or, better yet, a path to a better experience than what the property currently offers, then dig deeper as you may have uncovered a winner.

6.1.4. MULTIFAMILY

In the past, the multifamily asset class was considered more closely aligned with residential assets such as single-family homes. In recent years, however, the US has increasingly urbanized, and multifamily properties have become more institutional in nature with costly designs and vast amenities; they are increasingly owned by some of the country's largest institutional investors.

The multifamily asset class now accounts for the second largest share of institutional investor holdings, only lagging behind the office class. Multifamily assets are classified in a similar way to office buildings. The industry grades the properties as Class A, B, or C based on criteria such as age, quality, amenities, rent, and location among other factors.

- **Class A**: These properties are located in suburban locations and will likely offer resort-like settings complete with fountains, lavish pools, barbecue areas, and fitness centers. This class is best-in class and demands the highest rents.
- **Class B**: These are a step down from Class A and often have a "workforce housing" label, as they provide housing to median-wage owners.
- **Class C**: These properties are the lowest rated in the class structure. Class C properties are cheap to rent and have basic functional amenities. Often, these properties are older assets that have outdated building systems, designs, and finishes, or they may be in desperate need of maintenance and renovations.

As an asset class, multifamily spans across a wide spectrum of property types. It technically is defined as all buildings with at least two housing units, which are adjacent vertically or horizontally. Multifamily is also defined by shared physical systems, whether it be walls, roofs, heating and cooling, utilities, or amenities. This asset class can include townhomes, condominiums, and apartment complexes. For the purpose of this chapter, we'll focus only on apartments, as they're the most popular investment choices.

MIKE'S LAW #6

Invest Where You Have Market Knowledge or Analytical Advantage

Market inefficiency is the cornerstone advantage in choosing investments. Having "boots on the ground" intelligence gives investors inside information that the general public most likely does not have.

On the other hand, stock markets are the most efficient markets on earth. This means that information is available to everyone with a simple click on their iPhone. It's difficult to find value when everyone has the same knowledge. This investing law ensures that we have local knowledge in the market we are investing in and that we have insights and analytical data that give us an advantage over the competition.

Apartment buildings come in all shapes and sizes, ranging from dense, high-rise, and urban apartment buildings to resort-style complexes with swimming pools, fitness centers, and outdoor patios. They can be classified in terms of size and type as follows:

- **Low-rise or garden-style:** Two–four stories high and most typically found in suburban locations.
- **Mid-rise**: Five–nine stories.
- **High-rise:** Ten stories or higher.

Multifamily real estate has its own unique complexities and risk factors from an investment and risk-analysis perspective. Due to higher-than-average occupancies and lower volatility compared to other asset classes, it's often a popular choice to add in your investment portfolio. Apartment buildings have a lower cost of capital and wider availability of debt capital. Government-backed agencies, Fannie Mae and Freddie Mac, will lend on multifamily assets but not on other commercial real estate asset classes. During the recession, multifamily generally performed the best in class and lead the recovery. There is something to be said for the fact that people need a place to live no matter what the economic cycle we're experiencing.

While all commercial real estate asset classes have their pros and cons, some investors get caught up in being married to one asset class. Remain open to exploring other asset classes as they all have superior qualities to complement your Wall Street portfolio.

"I believe in being an innovator."

—WALT DISNEY

6.2. COMBINING ASSET CLASSES

There are benefits to combining different commercial real estate asset classes in your investment strategy. Each asset class, as we've seen, has unique characteristics such as leasing terms and fundamentals that work well together. Strategically placing multiple asset classes together will help your portfolio produce consistent higher returns and performance.

Let's take a look at an example of combining asset classes.

A well-known private commercial real estate fund took a smart approach by using an office building and a multi-family building to balance stability and growth within the fund. A typical office building leases to their tenants on three-to-five-year terms. Rent increases are negotiated in advance and are contractually locked in with an annual escalation fee between 3 percent and 4 percent. In other words, the tenant's lease rates will rise annually according to their negotiated escalation fee.

In the case of the fund we're discussing, they located an office building asset that had big upside, but was a risky purchase due its high vacancy. The building was a 50,000 square foot general office structure with a 50 percent vacancy—only 25,000 square feet was currently leased with paying tenants. Due to the high vacancy, the office building was purchased at a below-market price of only $7.5 million. After acquisition, the fund management was successful in leasing the building to 90 percent occupancy in four years. This was a great success for the fund.

Complementing the office building asset, the fund also invested in an apartment complex in the same geographic market. The current operations within the apartment asset were stable, and the tenants had shorter one-term leases. This short duration provided an opportunity to quickly raise the rental rates to match the rising market and test if improvements could generate even higher rental rates.

While the office building asset provided longer stable leases that lent stability to the investment portfolio, the apartment asset responded quickly to an improving market and provided stronger cash flow to the portfolio. Over the four years the fund held the investments, the assets earned an internal rate of return of 25 percent and a 2.5-times equity multiple and were less exposed to economic shock than either investment on their own.

Now that we have a good understanding of the assortment of commercial real estate types, it's important to see clearly how these assets are organized into investment funds. We'll learn why smaller, more entrepreneurial funds outperform the larger institutional real estate funds. Let's also find out ways to invest in these real estate funds to achieve your asset allocation strategy.

KEY TAKEAWAYS

- → While all commercial real estate asset classes have their pros and cons, some investors get caught up in being married to one asset class. Remain open to exploring other asset classes.
- → Market inefficiency is the cornerstone advantage in choosing good investments. Having "boots on the ground" intelligence gives investors inside information that the general public most likely does not have.

CHAPTER 7

DOES SIZE MATTER?

"If size mattered, the elephant would be king of the jungle."

—RICKSON GRACIE

Private commercial real estate, once considered a risky alternative investment, has gone mainstream. But how does this affect high-net-worth investors? In this chapter, we're going to discuss the difference between smaller private real estate funds and the larger institutional funds and how they affect investors. We touched upon this in section 4.3 in chapter 4, when we discussed what real estate options financial advisors typically offer you, and in section 5.1 in chapter 5, when we defined small commercial private real estate funds. Now we'll delve into it in depth, and unpack how your money may be served better by small funds rather than large, institutional players.

7.1. UNDERDOGS VS. THE BIG INSTITUTIONAL PLAYERS

The big institutional players are names you're probably familiar with: Blackstone Group, Starwood Capital, Lone Star Funds, Brookfield Asset Management, and Apollo Management. In 2019, Blackstone Group launched the largest private real estate fund ever recorded at $20 billion. This is $4.2 billion larger than their previous real estate fund in 2015. Blackstone's new fund gives it over $60 billion in buying power as the fund typically operates at $2 of debt for every $1 of equity. Starwood Capital's private real estate funds have raised over $31 billion since they got into commercial real estate investing. Most notably, Starwood sold the Baccarat Hotel to Chinese investors for a record amount of $230 million. That's $2 million per room.

These large players have become masters at raising capital from investors and for good reason. They've learned private real estate is a refuge from the volatility of Wall Street. It's hard to disrupt the world of big-name private real estate funds and their billion-dollar deals. They're celebrated in the headlines, amass huge funds, and scoop up trophy properties—but they may not be earning the best returns on their investments. These big-name funds can certainly validate the role private equity can play in commercial real estate and the wealth created for high-net-worth individuals. But in private real estate, does size really matter? What is the track record for small versus large real estate funds? We've crunched the numbers, and the results are surprising.

According to Prequin, a London-based data company that specializes in private equity reporting, the numbers tell an interesting story. The data was analyzed on large private real estate funds that made their first investment between the years 2005 and 2015. For funds with over $1 billion in assets, the average net internal rate of return (IRR) was 5.7 percent. For smaller funds with less than $200 million in assets, the net internal rate of return (IRR) was 11.2 percent. Smaller fund managers outperformed the big money by 96 percent![29]

So how do these underdogs run ahead of the pack?

A few thoughts first come to mind. These big-name funds act more like Wall Street mutual funds than entrepreneurial enterprises (which you'll see among the smaller funds). The name of the game is to raise as much capital as possible for ego and bragging rights, but they are also compensated by fees for assets under management. You may remember this from chapter 3: Wall Street and their large real estate fund friends thrive on large fees, and they're getting rich doing it.

But the one strategy that worries me most is the huge responsibility these fund managers have to place billions of dollars in capital under tight time constraints. When Black-

29 Michael Episcope, "How Smaller Private Real Estate Funds Can Generate Bigger Returns," *Forbes*, May 3, 2018, https://www.forbes.com/sites/forbesrealestatecouncil/2018/05/03/how-smaller-private-real-estate-funds-can-generate-bigger-returns/#70db673051fd.

stone raises $20 billion, the investors demand immediate returns. The investor money does not generate returns until placed in the market as new real estate assets in the fund. In a competitive market such as commercial real estate, buying $60 billion of real estate in a short time period is a risky and difficult proposition. This equates to bad and sloppy buying decisions. What do these managers care? They're getting paid on assets under management. Sound familiar?

According to the *Wall Street Journal*, large private commercial real estate funds launched in 2013 and 2014 still held $24.8 billion in investor money yet to be placed in real estate assets. And this problem is only going to get worse.[30] Prequin, a research and data firm, announced large funds' uninvested money increased to a record $333 billion in 2019, up from $134 billion at the end of 2012. According to a 2018 survey conducted by Prequin, 68 percent of large fund managers said it was more difficult to find attractive investments.[31] The former managing partner of Starwood Capital Group said, "A lot of firms have been sitting on their hands and not putting money to work, and that's dangerous."

Large private commercial real estate firms missing dead-

30 Konrad Putzier, "Real Estate Funds Have a Problem: Too Much Cash," *Wall Street Journal*, March 26, 2019, https://www.wsj.com/articles/real-estate-funds-have-a-problem-too-much-cash-11553607001.

31 "Prequin Fund Manager Outlook," PSERS.pa.org, 2018.

lines can either mean going back to investors and requesting an extension, or being forced to return their money. Pension funds, endowments, sovereign wealth funds, and other investors now have the issue of meeting their investment return goals. One particular fund raised substantial investment dollars from German investors to focus on American real estate assets in 2016. The fund managers told the investors that the money would be placed by 2018. As of 2019, the $570 million fund still has unspent capital and still struggles to meet its investment criteria.

As discussed, the difficulty of placing large amounts of capital drives fund managers to make costly mistakes. One example is a fund that has been purchasing properties in all cash and using less debt than originally defined in their investment strategy. This move will dramatically lower investment returns and force investors to make difficult decisions moving forward.

These large private commercial real estate funds argue that they can meet their obligations more easily than smaller funds because they invest globally and have so much capital that they can buy entire companies or portfolios. But is this really the investment strategy investors signed on for?

Smaller real estate funds can operate with big advantages and have a more "boots on the ground" mentality. These funds can scout for value in corners of the commercial real estate market neglected by the big-name funds, maintain price discipline, and execute flawlessly to maximize value and profits.

6.2. ADVANTAGES OF SMALL PRIVATE COMMERCIAL REAL ESTATE FUNDS

As a principal and co-founder of a small private commercial real estate fund, I've experienced firsthand how a small firm is able to deliver high returns to investors. In private real estate, smaller investment funds are really not underdogs at all. The smaller funds have a different investment strategy and play the game on many different levels. Smaller commercial real estate funds focus on investor returns and are not beholden to growing their assets under management for fees and their allegiance to shareholders (as opposed to the individual investors).

So what do smaller private real estate funds do differently?

6.2.1. TAKE ADVANTAGE OF INEFFICIENCY

There is inefficiency in the private markets. The lower end of the market is less efficient than the higher end of the market. This is a huge advantage for smaller real estate funds and enables smaller fund managers to deliver real active return on investment.

FUN FACT

The Seattle Kingdome was so expensive that the building wasn't paid off until 2015—a full fifteen years after it was demolished.

The "efficient market hypothesis" was coined by Professor Eugene Fama at the University of Chicago Booth School of Business.[32] The idea is that the more information available, the more efficient a market operates. In finance, the efficient market hypothesis asserts that financial markets, such as the stock market, are "informationally efficient." In today's investment world, the average investor can turn on a mobile phone or computer that provides up-to-date information that only Wall Street brokers enjoyed in the past. Information is free to anyone who wants it regarding publicly traded stocks, which makes stock markets a very efficient market. This means that an investor cannot consistently achieve returns in excess of average market returns on a risk-adjusted basis, given the information publicly available at the time the investment is made.

Smaller private real estate funds that focus on smaller deal sizes are more likely to find and capitalize on pricing mistakes or anomalies. These properties are not as obvious or desirable to a wide range of buyers. Valuations can be more subjective because they are based on local compa-

32 "Efficient Capital Markets: A Review of Theory and Empirical Work," Chicago Booth Business School, May 20, 2014.

rables and market conditions. These deals are done by buyers with different criteria and levels of expertise. This inefficiency in the market can widen the spread of bidding and asking prices that create opportunities for off-market properties.

A simple way to sum up an inefficient market is to think of it this way. Your friend who owns a building down the street just told you he's ready to retire and move to Florida. You may ask, "Are you selling everything and leaving it all behind?" The answer to this question gives you an unfair advantage to the general market. If your friend acknowledges he's going to sell his building, this becomes local knowledge no one else has the privilege of knowing. You could use this information and make an offer on the building before anyone else knows a thing. This is the definition of inefficient market knowledge.

Small real estate funds pride themselves on having the ability to identify opportunities in the market first and being able to act quickly to capture those opportunities. Commercial real estate still operates at a local level. We like to say, "Think Global, Invest Local." A big-name real estate fund may not have the boots on the ground to see these market opportunities. This not only makes it difficult for big funds to acquire good assets, but these funds also struggle in marketing and managing a property for better investment returns.

I will never forget sitting in my office thirteen years ago and receiving a call from an unusual number from South Beach Miami. It was the fund manager from a large private equity fund based in Miami, Florida. They'd heard that I did a lot of commercial real estate work around Fairfax, Virginia, and they had just acquired a building there *sight unseen*. They needed to know what type of tenants had been in the building in the past, how the tenants' utilities accounts were set up, if the building was set up for multiple tenants, etc. They had already purchased the building for more than $10 million and had *no* clue what they had really purchased or what they were going to do with it. This is crazy town.

My business partners and I were amazed that this could happen on two levels. How do these large funds conduct such little due diligence and spend no time understanding what they are buying? They should have made that phone call *before* they closed on the property! How would their investors feel if they knew how their investment dollars were being stewarded?

I told this same story to a senior commercial real estate broker at another firm. He laughed and said he saw this all the time. These fund managers and asset managers from all over the world will buy buildings in the Washington, DC, metro area and think they can't miss, without knowing anything about the property. Don't get me wrong—

the Washington, DC, metro market is pretty strong, and because of the dominant government presence, the local market is insulated from some of the larger economic issues that affect other markets. But it's arrogant to assume that anything you do will be successful as long as it's in a primary market; it is a terrible assumption.

Working in the local market allows us to know whether certain locations in our area have vacancy issues or if there are other factors not suitable for good investment choices. Wouldn't you want the fund manager responsible for investing your money to know this instead of sitting at a computer five hundred miles away? This story epitomizes why market inefficiency works if done right.

6.2.2. ELIMINATE LAYERS OF FEES

A real estate fund's size influences not only its strategic priorities, but also its ability to efficiently invest capital. For example, a large fund with billions of dollars to invest needs to rely on many platforms and other managers to deploy the funds. Big-name billion-dollar funds must partner with regional operators to invest these large sums of capital and maintain a healthy deal flow. These regional players do not work for free and can be quite expensive. This is the problem: these regional partners and large fund managers must get paid before the investors, and this drives down returns. Sound familiar to Wall Street?

MIKE'S LAW #7

Invest Where the Jobs Are

Demand creates value for our investments. Investing in high-growth areas with strong employment outlooks gives our investment choices the best chance for success. Not much can overcome an asset when there is a lack of demand. You can put lipstick on a pig, but it's still a pig.

Smaller funds credit success by a "hands-on approach" as an operator and manager. These funds do not pay outside operators or have joint venture partnerships. All of the profits made within these funds are shared with the investors.

This layer of double fees is one of the biggest reasons for the underperformance of large real estate funds. We learned earlier about the dire effect fees can have on your investment portfolio. There is no difference in this scenario; it's clear that the big-name real estate funds operate along the same business model as our friends on Wall Street. Investing with a smaller real estate fund means fewer middlemen and fewer people requiring a piece of the pie. This gives investors an edge to higher returns and performance to their portfolio.

6.2.3. ALIGNMENT OF INTERESTS

The interests of small real estate funds continue to be more closely aligned with their investors' interests. This interest level is especially important when principals of a small private commercial real estate fund invest their own money alongside their investors. It's not uncommon for smaller fund managers to place a large share of their net worth on the line and have considerable money invested within the fund.

In Prequin's most recent survey of institutional large funds, 72 percent see high price valuations as a key factor facing the industry in 2019.[33] While good deals in private equity real estate are still available, it takes out-of-the-box thinking to find and profit from them. In recent years, the smaller funds have delivered up to double the return on investment as compared to their larger counterparts.

There are many quality small private real estate funds, but the industry is not set up to easily find them. Instead, the industry reverts back to traditional Wall Street thinking. Financial advisors routinely recommend large funds to investors and note they are best in class. These large institutional funds are typically the only funds most financial advisors have access to provide to clients. The fact is they are only best in class when compared to *other* large funds.

33 Swaraj Singh Dhanjal, "Asset Valuation Is Biggest Concern for Institutional Investors," Livemint.com, April 21, 2019, https://www.livemint.com/companies/news/asset-valuation-is-biggest-concern-for-institutional-investors-in-2019-report-1555872032564.html.

Investors have a better chance of diversifying their investment portfolios by asking their financial advisors to help them find high-quality performing smaller funds. These funds don't have marquee brands, but the performance of the smaller funds speak for themselves. The inherent problem still resides: financial advisors most likely are not compensated on these recommendations, and the Wall Street's conflict of interest with their clients continues.

After discussing this issue with a few of the top small-fund performers, Scott Munchel of Red Fox Capital comments, "What I'm seeing is that investors are challenging their consultants and advisors to find them alternative investments that outperform the baseline norms or the household names. So I think we are seeing a shift away from some of the big names and a significant shift away from open-minded core and into value-add emerging managers."

The small private commercial real estate funds are often difficult to find for the average investor. These funds are reserved for VIP high-net-worth clients and rarely advertise their offerings. In order to discover these funds, it's necessary to work with an appropriate financial advisor or directly with the real estate fund. We'll discuss in the next chapter techniques on how to identify these opportunities and exactly which fund fits your investment portfolio for maximum results.

KEY TAKEAWAYS

- → Size matters in private commercial real estate investment funds. Smaller funds with less than $200 million in assets outperform larger investment funds on average by 5.5 percent net internal rate of return.
- → The large household funds act more like Wall Street mutual funds than entrepreneurial enterprises.
- → Large real estate funds thrive on high fees, and they're getting rich doing it.
- → Smaller real estate funds can operate with advantages while exploiting value gaps in the market neglected by the larger funds.

CHAPTER 8

FINDING A COMMERCIAL REAL ESTATE FUND THAT FITS YOUR GOALS

"If everyone is thinking alike, then somebody isn't thinking."

—GENERAL GEORGE PATTON

Not all funds are created equal. Within private real estate investing, assets are typically sorted into four primary strategy categories based on investment strategies and perceived risk. These are not to be confused with the asset classes we discussed in an earlier chapter; these categories can describe any of the commercial real estate asset classes but, as you'll see, categorize the assets into risk tolerance and potential return respectively.

Investors should consider the level of risk they're willing to take and how long they are willing to wait before they begin receiving returns. Some investors may focus on long-term gains that have promising yields but little to no liquidity, while others may want to generate steady income that will offer more frequent dividends.

To achieve these specific investor goals, real estate fund managers focus on these four primary strategy categories: core, core plus, value add, and opportunistic. Each category delivers a different point of risk versus return and requires different types of leverage. Moving among these strategies is like stepping up the ladder in terms of taking on more risk and, in theory, being compensated for that risk with a higher return.

8.1. CORE

Core investments are considered the least risky because they involve steady, income-producing properties that are in prime locations in major markets. The properties also have no structural issues and enjoy full or high occupancy with high-credit tenants on long-term leases. These are Class A properties with steady income streams. For a landlord, what's not to like?

The desirability for these types of properties warrants low leverage—typically between 30 percent and 50 percent—and they are a perfect fit in a blue-chip portfolio that delivers a steady stream of income. The reason for low leverage with core is that it's simply not conducive to the use of much leverage given its low unleveraged growth. Leveraging core assets adds little to leveraged returns so it typically adds more risk than return.

The role of these core assets is to behave like a high-yield bond with little downside risk to principal investors. Typically, returns in this sector are around 5 percent to 7 percent annually. The offset to the stability of the assets is that these types of investments generally do not offer much potential for growth.

8.2. CORE PLUS

Core plus investments are held for both income and growth. They have similar characteristics to core, but have more potential for upside appreciation. A few more risks, such as the age or condition of the property, a dip in tenant credit, or less-than-ideal location, allow for more upside with proper management. Moreover, the property could have a high proportion of leases up for renewal. While core investors see this as a threat to steady income, core plus investors might see this as an opportunity to increase rents and increase yield.

The unleveraged returns of core plus assets are high enough

to justify the use of leverage to increase leveraged returns. Leverage is typically limited in order to limit risk and preserve the overall risk reward balance of a core plus profile. Average leveraged returns on these assets range from a net of 8 percent to 12 percent annually and are typically leveraged between 50 percent to 70 percent.

8.3. VALUE ADD

These properties take a step up the ladder risk and find themselves in the middle ground between conservative core and high-risk opportunistic. Investors who are looking to take on more risk to achieve high returns and are willing to defer gains should invest in either value-add or opportunistic properties.

These assets generally have a problem that needs fixing, such as leasing to improve significant vacancy, renovation, or retenanting to improve the quality of the rent roll. The fund usually acquires the asset with a specific business plan to improve this underutilized asset.

Value-add properties may require improvements that need a more complex business model to achieve higher returns. An example would be a shopping center that has lost an anchor tenant, such as a grocery store or other big-box tenant. The fund will have an opportunity to purchase the property at a discount given the absence of an anchor. If the fund manager has an effective business plan to reposition the anchor space and bring new tenants to the property that would improve the overall shopping experience, the new owner can make substantial profit. The business plan could also discover that breaking the large anchor space into smaller spaces could achieve higher return on the investment. Remember, bigger is not always better. Reformatting a former Food Lion grocery store into a combination of a Trader Joe's and Bed Bath & Beyond would bring a better shopping experience and would drive more traffic to the center. A well-executed business plan could turn a value-add property into a core plus fairly easily.

Nearly all of the value-add investor's returns will come in the form of appreciation, with no expectation of cash flow for at least twenty-four to thirty-six months. Value add properties have the potential to be more lucrative than core and core plus strategies with the right kind of physical upgrades, better management, added services, or more effective marketing.

The targeted returns for a value-add property average between 13 percent and 18 percent annually, and they are typically leveraged between 60 percent to 75 percent. Unleveraged returns on value-add assets are now high enough to entice the additional use of leverage to further enhance leveraged returns. In addition, retenanting and repositioning strategies, as described above, can often be mostly capitalized through additional leverage that is funded by the senior lender post-closing, as stated in the business plan. In industry jargon, this is referred to as "future funding."

8.4. OPPORTUNISTIC

Opportunistic assets are the final rung on the ladder of risk. These deals are generally extreme turnaround situations, adaptive reuse, or even new ground-up development. The unifying strategy is that investors are willing to take outsized risks and put in higher upfront costs to achieve outsized returns.

Other issues with opportunistic properties could be a major vacancy, structural issues, or financial distress. Sometimes referred to as "distressed assets," opportunistic strategies may involve acquiring foreclosed assets from banks or servicers or acquiring the senior debt at a discount from banks or servicers with plans of eventual foreclosure.

Opportunistic assets were plentiful during the recession, as bold investors stepped in to buy properties in distress at steep discounts. In some cases, opportunistic deals require special expertise to execute the turnaround or patience to wait out a downturn in the market to effect a value-add strategy once tenant demand begins again. The unifying strategy is that investors are willing to take outsized risks and put in higher upfront costs to achieve outsized returns.

FUN FACT

In 2007, Leona Helmsley, the real estate magnate and hotelier, left her dog Trouble over $12 million in her will.

It's interesting that opportunistic new construction projects might eventually deliver core properties that attract high-profile tenants. However, getting there takes years of labor, management-intensive development work, and substantial market risk before the first rent checks appear. Given these risk characteristics, there is typically a very high return threshold to meet before investors should consider making opportunistic investments.

The targeted returns for these assets should generate above 20 percent annually and typically leverage 70 percent or more. If successful, these investments can be super profitable. Due to the distressed nature of the opportunistic asset strategy, they are often not eligible for much or any leverage upon acquisition. If you acquired a note, you essentially bought the leveraged part of the deal with a strategy to convert into a low-basis unleveraged asset. The broad range is due to the fact that opportunistic strategies are highly specific case dependent. Opportunistic assets may also start with little to no leverage but find their way to leverage or increased leverage as the business plan develops.

For example, a fund acquires a 100,000 square foot vacant

retail building for $3 million or $30/square foot, all cash, that could potentially be valued at $18 million or $180/ square foot with a stable triple net (NNN) tenant on a long-term lease. However, the tenant will require $7 million of tenant improvements and capital improvements in order to attract them to the building. With a signed lease in hand, the fund could approach a lender, pledge the unleveraged building as collateral, and obtain a loan for the entire $7 million required to perform the improvements to install the tenant. Once the tenant takes occupancy, the fund now has a core plus asset.

8.5. CHOOSING THE RIGHT STRATEGY

When picking the right category for investment, investors should consider the time horizon to risk tolerance. Below, we've given you a guideline to assist in your investment strategy.

TIME HORIZON	RISK TOLERANCE		
	CONSERVATIVE	MODERATE	AGGRESSIVE
0–5 years	Core	Core	Core Plus
5–10 years	Core	Core Plus	Opportunistic/ Value Add
10–20 years	Core Plus	Core Plus/Value Add	Opportunistic/ Value Add

> **MIKE'S LAW #8**
>
> **Use Leverage and Debt Conservatively**
>
> Leverage is a magical component to creating great returns on investment. However, using leverage irresponsibly is destructive and not encouraged. A simple example is the average homeowner in the United States purchasing homes they could not afford. When valuations and interest rates changed, the debt coverage or mortgage could not be met. Millions of homeowners lost their properties by not managing their debt in a responsible manner.

It's also important for investors to understand the risk and return relationship when discussing the four different types of real estate investment strategies. The level of the return should be commensurate with the amount of risk.

When it comes to value-add and opportunistic deals, you also need to keep in mind the expertise of the fund manager and their ability to create and execute a business plan, as this can be critical to the success of the project.

A well-balanced commercial real estate portfolio may include some or even all of these different investment categories depending on the risk tolerance of the individual investor.

Now that we've covered all the different types of commercial real estate assets, fund types, and specific strategies for each type, it's time to learn how to analyze and conduct appropriate due diligence on both the real estate operators/ fund managers and the underlying real estate asset itself. Bear with me in the next chapter as we get a bit legal and technical when it comes to due diligence. Feel free to come back to the chapter later if you're not ready to conduct background diligence on a specific real estate asset now.

KEY TAKEAWAYS

- → Investors should consider the level of risk they're willing to take and how long they are willing to wait before they begin to receive returns.
- → It's important to understand the risk and return relationship among the different types of real estate investment strategies.
- → A well-balanced commercial real estate portfolio may include some or even all of the different investment categories.
- → The investor should carefully consider the sponsor before investing in any deal, but the riskier the investment, the more you must rely on the sponsor to be able to deliver on their plan in order to achieve the projected returns.

CHAPTER 9

DUE DILIGENCE

"The leading rule for the lawyer, as for the man of every calling, is diligence."

—ABRAHAM LINCOLN

Have you just met the next Bernie Madoff? Madoff was the financial advisor who confessed to operating the world's largest Ponzi scheme. He stole over $64.8 billion from over 4,800 trusting clients. Madoff destroyed lives driven by greed and dishonesty. This makes due diligence an important part of all decision-making.

Warren Buffett so eloquently stated: "Only when the tide goes out do you discover who's been swimming naked." We all tend to make decisions about our financial advisors and real estate fund managers based on their reputation in the community, how credible they seem, and if they understand their business. Even Alan Greenspan, the longest-serving Chairman of the Board of Governors of the Federal Reserve, testified to Congress: "Rarely did anyone question my tactics for fear of looking competent." But the Great Recession uncovered some questionable businesses as the "tide went out."

- 2009: Bernie Madoff's $65 billion Ponzi scheme.
- 2009: Allen Stanford gathered $8 billion in a Ponzi scheme by falsely promising the safety and security of certificates of deposit.
- 2010: Chase, GMAC, Bank of America, and others were caught performing nonjudicial foreclosures.
- 2010: Countrywide's CEO, Angelo Mozilo, misrepresented company data to appease investors. These investors consisted of many Americans who held mutual funds or pensions.
- 2012: Several investment banks, including Chase and Barclays, were intentionally manipulating The London Interbank Offered Rate (LIBOR), a benchmark interest rate, affecting trillions of dollars of loans.
- 2012: HSBC was caught money laundering for Mexican drug cartels and countries known to shelter terrorists, such as Iran.
- 2016: Over 5,000 Wells Fargo employees knowingly opened more than 3.5 million fake bank accounts. That means 5,000 employees thought it was perfectly fine to create fraudulent accounts to inflate performance numbers.

It can seem a bit adventurous to invest with a small private commercial real estate firm. But, as you can see from the examples above, everything is fraught with risk, even those products you think are safe bets. The key is proper due diligence. With the right due diligence, your investment portfolio will thank you time and again.

This chapter will deal with the smart questions you should ask when choosing the right fund, and what you need to investigate when finding assets that align with your investment strategy. It's not our intention to uncover a thief in the night like the colorful examples above; rather, it's more about finding the right partner for your investment success.

9.1. FINDING THE RIGHT REAL ESTATE FUND MANAGER

When we first look at any investment opportunity, it's an exciting time with the promise of high returns. But it's unlikely that any investment will play out exactly as the pro forma plan suggests. The issue with relying on pro forma projections to make decisions in a real estate investment is that anything can look great with a few window-dressing tweaks. Some of the investments will outperform projections, some will be close, and others will lose. So the challenge of the investor is to find out which opportunities will meet or exceed expectations.

Private real estate funds build financial models and make

assumptions that their projections can be achieved. But, just as you'll find among Wall Street analysts, some less scrupulous will build models with aggressive and often unattainable projections to attract investors and capital. Projecting real estate outcomes is not an exact science, with hundreds of variables going into the financial model. The fund manager controls these variables and makes the final call when developing these models. It's very easy to tweak a few variables to change the outcome on any deal. When playing with financial models, it's quite easy to make any deal work on paper.

Finding a real estate fund manager who behaves reasonably and responsibly is critical to your success in investing with private commercial real estate. The manager is the person responsible for determining the price to pay for an asset, how to build value, appropriate capital structure, how to correct course when things go wrong, and when to exit the property. A good quality in a real estate manager is being realistic and thoughtful about their assumptions. Asking the right questions of a fund manager during due diligence is necessary to understand if their investment strategy aligns with your personal risk profile. It's just like a job interview, and you're hiring a fund manager to be a good steward of your capital and a good partner.

"You can tell a lot about a fellow's character by his way of eating jellybeans."

—RONALD REAGAN

Let's examine a list of questions you should ask any commercial real estate fund manager to fully understand their approach, ethics, and potential performance.

1. ARE THE FINANCIAL MODEL ASSUMPTIONS ACCURATE?

The easiest way to start your interview process is to evaluate and question all the assumptions made on the financial model. Projections are only as good as the inputs, and every one of them is at the discretion of the fund manager. How a fund manager underwrites a real estate deal is a great way to determine how aggressive or conservative they will behave.

The first thing to look for is the projected internal rate of return (IRR). If you research the top-ten opportunities in the same industry and the IRR projections range between 16 percent and 19 percent, what is the chance another fund manager can achieve 30 percent IRR? One lesson I learned early in my investment career was to be sensitive to high returns. When something looks too good to be true, it often is. Any investment with promises of 30 percent and plus annual returns is something to be very concerned about and most likely not true.

The market is generally efficient, so beware of aggressive marketing techniques. I once attended a legal compliance seminar in Los Angeles with Gene Trowbridge, the legal authority on private commercial real estate fund investment. The hotel conference room was filled with successful real estate fund managers from across the country. It was quite alarming to hear some of these fund managers speak out loud about their marketing practices. I'll never forget a fund manager from Louisiana that placed ads in local newspapers touting his fund's investment success and high rate of returns. This was an illegal practice prior to the Jobs Act of 2016, but, more importantly, he was misleading investors about their performance. A solid private commercial real estate fund would not partake in these practices.

Location, location, location.

How does the location of the property and its physical attributes stand up to other opportunities and competition? Make sure while evaluating these other opportunities that the assets are compared as apples to apples. Commercial real estate can change dramatically block by block, so comparing the property to one that is ten miles away may not be appropriate. I've seen property valuations fluctuate dramatically within a one-mile radius.

What rental rates do they need to achieve compared to the market? If competitive properties are achieving $23 per square foot rental rates, why does the fund manager believe they can achieve $25 per square foot? This is a common input variable fund managers exploit. A good fund manager will explain his assumptions of rental rates and comparables in the market.

I once had a consulting client looking to build a commercial real estate portfolio. He was a technology executive with little to no experience in commercial real estate. The ambitious executive walked into my office one morning with a giant smile on his face. "I've got a winner," he said. "What do you think?" It didn't take long to see the problem.

The author of his assumptions had an aggressive 25 percent annual rental escalation while the traditional market would charge 3 percent. Now this is a ridiculous but true example of what happens. How many tenants do you know who would allow their rent to appreciate 25 percent a year over a five-year term? I would guess, not one.

It's a good practice to invest in deals with assumptions that are easily achievable. What is the fund manager's exit cap rate assumption? And is there a built-in cushion for expanding cap rate? This is another area that is very easy to exploit. Changing a cap rate can make a financial model look great. Generally speaking, exit cap rates should be twenty-five to fifty basis points higher than the current market rate to account for risk. Make sure that the value created is not financially engineered.

Good fund managers create value by increasing net operating income. How are they going to achieve this? Net operating income is impacted most by occupancy and rental rates. What is their assumed growth rate of revenue, and how do they determine it? What is their terminal occupancy rate? Every financial model has an occupancy assumption at stabilization. Make sure the property is in line with the market, or slightly below it. For example, if the market has a 15 percent vacancy rate, it's unrealistic for the manager to assume 100 percent occupancy, and that will significantly impact both the net operating income and the ultimate valuation of the property.

How does the manager treat expenses, such as property taxes, and are they applying a realistic inflation rate to all of the expenses? Property tax increases can have a big impact on the bottom line. Make sure the fund is resetting them based on the new purchase price and not using historical figures. The taxes will go up, and sometimes substantially.

Most importantly, what is the fund manager's business plan for the property, and do you think it's realistic? Use a common-sense approach. Could a Class A property also be a home to low-income tenants? A business plan should be easy to understand and make sense intuitively.

2. HOW MUCH MONEY ARE YOU INVESTING?

Alignment is one of the most important things, in my opinion. A fund manager should be investing a significant amount of his or her own capital right along with you and other investors. The bulk of the fund manager's earnings should come from investment returns and not transactional fees... Remember chapter 3 on Wall Street fees? "Skin in the game" by your fund manager ensures they are motivated by asset performance. You want them to win when you win and lose when you lose.

3. WHAT IS THE COMPETITIVE ADVANTAGE IN THE MARKET?

What does the fund manager believe is their best talent and expertise in the market? If they don't have a competitive advantage, then why invest with them? A competitive advantage is typically something quantifiable. For example, if their competitive advantage is in sourcing opportunities, then how many deals do they look at before an asset is picked, and where do they find them? If their advantage is in operations, then they should be able to benchmark themselves against an industry standard.

If you come across a fund manager that may not necessarily have the top-in-class expertise, it is possible for the fund manager to team with other commercial real estate operators. Our fund once had a wonderful opportunity to develop a multifamily Class A apartment complex in an opportunity zone. Our team does have extensive development experience, just not a deep bench with multifamily. We teamed with an expert in multifamily, and the project was quite successful. Don't cut your fund manager short unnecessarily; there are emerging managers without tons of experience, but who are able to build great teams and produce great returns.

4. HOW IS MY CAPITAL PROTECTED IN A DOWN MARKET?

Does the private real estate fund have a strategy and track record that makes you feel comfortable? Do they consistently beat their own projections? How much leverage do they use? Some points to consider include the following:

You should ask about their underwriting and how they take into account a potentially rising interest rate market and a rising cap rate environment. You don't have to agree with them on which way interest rates are going, but every financial model should account for how to deal with this because there is real risk. It's always important in real estate to protect the downside.

How much leverage does the fund manager use? Used responsibly, leverage enhances returns. But beware of deals that are financially engineered with mezzanine debt and preferred equity.

Does the fund personally guarantee loans? Personally guaranteeing loans can be catastrophic for a fund manager and private real estate investors. The risk to the investor is if the manager has overexposed themselves on these guarantees, they may be making decisions on selling a property either to reduce that exposure or to be able to buy another property that may have better returns but that the individual investor may not be part of. The manager may be making these decisions based on what is best for him and not on what is best for that particular investment. Moreover, investors should find out if and how much the manager will charge the deal for a personal guarantee.

5. HOW CAN THE DEAL LOSE MONEY?

All deals have the potential to lose money. It's just not common for a fund manager to address this in the marketing materials. A good manager will have thought this through, so listen for a well-reasoned and sincere answer.

Ask them for a stress test model to better understand the "what if" scenarios. Again, question the assumptions in the financial model. The easiest question is the exit cap rate. A good manager will assume a higher cap rate at exit to account for potentially rising interest rates, the age of the building, and potentially lower lease terms. For example, if the market cap rate today is 6 percent, then the exit cap rate should be between 6.25 percent and 6.5 percent. If the fund manager doesn't follow this rule, then the other assumptions may not be realistic as well.

There are certain circumstances where a fund may acquire several smaller properties at higher cap rates and look to package them together with the idea to sell them as a portfolio to larger funds. In many cases, these larger funds are willing to pay for the ease of someone else doing the work to package multiple assets and pay a lower cap rate to acquire them all at once.

The investor should never be afraid to ask the manager questions and press them on these assumptions, listen to the manager's responses, and then verify what they are being told before investing.

6. WHAT WAS YOUR WORST DEAL AND WHAT DID YOU LEARN?

Every commercial real estate fund manager has a bad deal in their past. It's your decision to determine if it was a flawed business plan or the function of a bad market. Did the manager communicate to investors during this period? This is important, because how they treat the investors during bad times is an indicator of their integrity. While no fund manager is obligated to go above and beyond what they state in their documents, an honest fund manager will have done something to make amends.

7. HOW IS THE FUND TEAM INCENTIVIZED?

Making sure the fund team is aligned through performance is important. You should ask how the fund retains team members and what their retention rate is for key team members.

Conflicts of interest are prevalent in this industry, and min imizing them is important. One way is by making sure a majority of the team's compensation is based on performance and not on the transaction. Also make sure the team that's in place today is the same one that was responsible for delivering the manager's historical returns.

8. WHAT IS INCLUDED IN THE FUND'S FEE?

Fees can erode a deal's return, as we've learned earlier in this book. Make sure the deal is not stacked with lots of fees. Ask about each fee throughout the structure of the deal. Sometimes, these fees are buried in other LLCs below the investment entity. Ask for an organizational chart and then inquire about fees in each and every one.

6.2. USING PRIVATE PLACEMENT MEMORANDUMS TO EVALUATE REAL ESTATE DEALS

Each and every private investment fund should come with its own private placement memorandum (PPM). A PPM can also be referred to as a private offering document or a confidential offering memorandum.

These documents look intimidating, with pages filled with legal phrases and disclaimers. After reviewing a PPM, you'll be convinced that investing would be a crazy thing to do. I'll never forget our fund's first PPM—there must have been a hundred pages on why you should not invest and a compilation of creative risk factors that only a team of highly paid attorneys could think of. For example, there was a clause in our PPM that stated you could lose your entire investment because of the War in Iraq. The asset was an office building in *Virginia*, and my assumption was the property would be highly unlikely to be affected by the War in Iraq; at the very least, it was highly unlikely investors would lose their entire investment. Just be prepared for outlandish language.

However, if you know how to read a PPM, you can learn a lot not only about the individual asset or fund, but also about the professionalism of your fund manager. Most investors never really read the PPM, but rely on referrals, marketing materials, face-to-face meetings, and phone conversations to make their investment decisions. Generally, this strategy works fine. It's when things go wrong that it's good to know what the PPM says and how the legal structure is established.

The investment research information available for public

investments, such as annual reports, 10ks, and 10Qs, isn't available in a private real estate opportunity. Investors use the PPM to become familiar with the terms of the private investment and the necessary information to evaluate the opportunity. So reviewing the PPM is one important step in the due diligence process.

First, you should pay particular attention to any capitalized terms. The fund issuers may define terms differently, so don't assume to understand the meaning of these terms without making reference to the accurate definition in the referenced PPM document. For example, Net Asset Value (NAV) may be defined by one fund as the equity portion of the investment once liquidated, while another fund may be referring to the entire property value including the debt. In this example, a 2 percent management fee on NAV of the equity will be far less than a 1 percent fee charged on the NAV of the property, assuming moderate leverage is used on the property.

6.2.1. DIFFERENT SECTIONS OF A PPM

PPMs vary according to the fund and the particular style of the issuer. PPMs can also be different depending on the size of the offering and the number and type of investors being solicited, but each PPM should at least contain the five sections outlined below.

1. Executive Summary

The executive summary is a summary of the investment. It usually includes the investment thesis, pricing, minimum subscription amount, investor qualifications, disclosure of management fees, and a brief discussion of the fund issuer's governing documents.

Be aware of disclaimers that allow the fund management to have too much latitude or discretion, and pay close attention to the conflicts of interest. The executive summary should be in harmony with what's stated in the marketing materials and represented by the fund's management team. Always look for inconsistencies and contradictions in language.

2. Investment Strategy

The investment strategy section describes a thorough explanation of the fund's investment strategy, process, and criteria, as well as its deal flow sourcing and exit strategy. This section also includes a description of the fund's key competitive advantages and resources in its specified markets. It will also discuss the industry, state, and geographical focus of the investment.

Investors should review this section to learn how the fund intends to achieve its targeted results and to assess whether the investment strategy supports the fund's objective.

MIKE'S LAW #9

Hire Honest and Competent Advisors and Management Teams

All investors must trust their financial stewards. With today's financial world full of scandal and mistrust, this is imperative. Most investment advisors are honest, but sometimes these managers are pressured into financially engineering spreadsheets to make the returns look better than actual. It's very easy to tweak numbers, cap rates, and assumptions to make managers look more favorable.

Investors need to analyze the assumptions the investment advisors present and make educated decisions. Often, red flags present themselves, and if your gut tells you to investigate, you should dive deeper into due diligence.

Investment strategies that are well reasoned and clearly written will provide investors with information they'll need to make a fully informed investment decision. An offering with an investment strategy that is vague, unclear, or that does not make sense is probably an offering that should be avoided.

3. Management and Experience

The management and experience section contains the biographical and background information about the fund's principals and key employees. It provides a detailed overview of the fund's history and how it has succeeded.

This section often provides the fund's investment manager's track record, which is generally presented in a record table format, outlining past fund sizes, vintage years, and IRR performance. A more robust track record will contain additional performance statistics, such as realized/unrealized IRR and actual/projected gross multiples.

The success of an investment will be dependent on the management team, so it's important the team has a background and experience to implement the investment strategy. Prior experience successfully managing similar investments supports the proposition that the management team is capable of implementing the investment strategy with positive results.

4. Summary of Principal Terms

The summary of principal terms outlines the organization of the company, what fees investors pay, what expenses the company will bear, how profits will be split, and a thorough summary of the business plan.

A careful analysis of the summary of principal terms should provide most of the information necessary to fully comprehend the investment offer. The investor can refer to the PPM section in the document for further details if anything doesn't seem accurate or requires more information.

5. Risk Factors

Risk factors is the section that will truly make your eyes glaze over. Remember the crazy War in Iraq reference? Few investors need to be advised that "in the event of war, no assurance can be given that the investment will meet its stated goals."

This section is important because it outlines the factors that make the investment risky or speculative. While there are certain risks that are present in nearly all investments, such as civil unrest, bankruptcy, and natural disasters, investors should pay attention to those risks that are unique to the investment opportunity given the nature of the fund issuer, its investment plans, and the trends within the fund's industry.

Besides the risks inherent in the investment, there are risks associated with the offering entity and the management team. Conflicts of interest could be of significance. Certain conflicts to consider include the following:

- *Fees and expenses*: Shifting expenses from management to the investor, charging management salaries and overhead to the fund, allocating transaction fees to the fund and not co-investors are a few examples.
- *Transaction with affiliates*: Affiliations with management, such as management acting as a creditor or lender to the fund, or the fund acquires an investment from a management affiliate.

- *Competing funds*: Management launches a new fund with the same strategy as an earlier fund, creating a conflict between allocations of investments between funds.

6.3. HOW FUNDS CONDUCT DUE DILIGENCE ON ASSETS

"Whenever you do a thing, act as if the world were watching."

—THOMAS JEFFERSON

It's important to also consider how a fund conducts due diligence on particular assets. It's always exciting after many months pursuing a commercial real estate property and finally winning the contract battle and becoming the purchaser. This is when the serious work begins, and professional and organized funds will have a process.

Time is of the essence. You've probably heard this phrase before, but it is a critical phrase in this case because most commercial real estate purchase agreements may only give contract purchasers thirty to sixty days to conduct due diligence. This time period, also called the "Study Period," is the time to discover any unexpected issues with the property that may potentially yield post-acquisition surprises.

Investors should ask the fund's management exactly how assets are researched and vetted before they're acquired. A full documentation process on the property's condition allows the fund's team to determine if management is able to rework spaces, update amenities, or enhance aspects of the building that will substantially improve the tenant's living or working conditions. A business plan is then created to address these issues, as well as increase the property's earnings, long-term value, and the return of investment for the investors.

The due diligence process gives the buyer full access to the property for a comprehensive understanding of the commercial real estate asset. Typically, the buyer and seller of the property agree to a timeline for the buyer to obtain all the information they feel relevant prior to ownership and negotiate an agreement to give the buyer access to the property while the purchase agreement is being negotiated. The buyer will most likely negotiate more time, while the seller will negotiate the shortest time possible. The standard purchase agreement allows sixty days to close on the property, with thirty days being a due diligence study period.

The buyer will be asked to make a security earnest deposit with the seller to confirm their intent to purchase the property. This deposit is traditionally not at risk during the study period. If the buyer uncovers any substantial new issues during the due diligence period, there's a window of opportunity to discuss these issues with the seller. Buyers that value their underwriting acumen and deal-making reputation in the commercial real estate community will want to avoid adjusting the purchase price unless significant problems are discovered. This tactic is referred to "retrading" a deal and is frowned upon in the industry.

If critical issues are uncovered, they need to be addressed in a timely fashion. Buyers should have their entire team engaged during the due diligence process, including lenders, general contractors, architects, and designers. A professional fund manager will go beyond the minimum hurdles during the due diligence period to investigate five key categories, as given below.

6.3.1. OPERATIONAL DUE DILIGENCE

It's important to ensure that the designed business plan on the property is achievable during due diligence. The first step is to hire and vet the professional team on the project. Selecting the best property manager that will fulfill the fund's vision and values is generally one of the first decisions made during the process. The fund's manager will interview the property's existing management and leasing team to verify their knowledge of the asset, their local market competence, and their synergy with the tenants. The fund manager will also interview a network of experts to ensure the property is being served by the best possible management and leasing teams, as the fund's requirements extend beyond just operating the property efficiently.

Second, a marketing plan is developed. The marketing plan

is to rebrand the property, which can mean revitalizing a community feel among tenants, improving the quality of tenants or improving a property to the point where it can compete with or exceed the performance of previously superior assets. The fund shares the vision with the property manager, and the team works with them to implement the defined strategies. The fund expects that this work, when done correctly, will result in higher rents or yields on the property.

6.3.2. FINANCIAL DUE DILIGENCE

An essential due diligence step is to investigate the property's cash flow to ensure the income and expenses match the seller's representations and to determine if the property's rent roll is sustainable. A few audit processes include the following:

Lease Audits: Most purchase agreements require the seller of a commercial real estate investment to provide access to all leases for the property. The fund team, in conjunction with the legal team and other affiliated parties, compares actual hard-copy leases to the rent roll to measure accuracy.

This is a tedious process. For example, lease audits could involve five hundred residential leases with an apartment property or sixty commercial leases within an office building asset. It's important to verify that move-in and move-out dates, agreed-upon rental rates, renewal options, security deposits, and other additional charges and stipulations are consistent with what the seller has represented.

Contract Audits: An audit to review existing service contracts is next. The property may have agreements in place with cable and internet providers, landscaping, snow removal, office equipment services and technicians, and third-party maintenance providers. The fund's team studies these contracts to better understand whether to continue these contracts as the property's new owner. If other available providers offer better services for a lower price, the fund identifies if these current contracts can be renegotiated or canceled.

Rent Roll Analysis: The fund analyzes the timing of expirations and associated rollover schedules, as well as any termination, renewal, or relocation options that might be associated with the tenants. Some tenants might have special options in their lease, so it's important to know about these special options prior to taking ownership.

In a multifamily asset, ensuring that all existing leases are more heavily weighted to expire during the strong leasing season is a good idea. This allows the fund the ability to increase rental rates on new leases while demand is higher than other times of the year and allows the fund's management the broadest market possible to fill any vacancies.

Cost Analysis: Analysis of historical operations provides valuable insight on what expenses should be expected once the fund begins operating the property. When performing this analysis, the fund looks to find areas to save money. For example, is the property overpaying staff? Can a more affordable insurance policy be implemented? Are the property owners paying for unnecessary items? It's easy to assume you can operate a property more efficiently than the previous owner. This is commonly referred to as "buyer's bias" and is not always correct.

A fund can eliminate a "buyer's bias" by comparing the property to similar property operations. Using comparable properties the fund underwrites, the fund will build an ever-growing database to benchmark prospective acquisitions based on geographic location, vintage, construction type, and number of units. The fund management can then gauge properties across these different metrics to prevent "buyer's bias" and develop a realistic budget.

Market Analysis: A market study is performed to estimate future rents the fund feels can be charged by studying similar property locations, finishes, amenities, and other variables. When a fund makes a value-add investment, the fund should project what can be charged over current rent after upgrading interior spaces, amenities, parking, etc., and the fund can consider how repositioning the asset will enhance its value at sale.

6.3.3. LEGAL DUE DILIGENCE

The fund's legal team takes every step possible to ensure all entitlements and obligations are identified on the property. These can include the following:

Title Transfer: The property's title policy stipulates all collateral that falls under the owner's authority. The fund should utilize both internal and external counsel to study the title policies of prospective property and ensure that no parties have outstanding negative issues on the policy that would affect ownership.

Survey Report: A survey report should be ordered to make sure the fund has the most up-to-date information possible on the property site. The report allows the fund to better understand the land parcel, any site access rights to adjacent land parcels, the boundaries of the lot, and any required setbacks to consider in a development opportunity.

The property's current zoning designation should also be assessed for current and development opportunity.

6.3.4. PHYSICAL DUE DILIGENCE

The fund will engage structural consultants during due diligence to understand any engineering implications before formally purchasing the property. The purchase agreement offers complete access to the property for more thorough inspections than were possible before negotiating the intent to purchase, and it allows the fund to obtain a range of reports to determine budgets.

During the physical due diligence, the property is examined in depth. A certified engineer inspects the property's current condition and reviews its original plans and specifications to determine whether the property was built according to code. The inspection also extends to "the bones" of the property to make sure they are structurally sound.

A property appraiser will review the property's historical operations, calculate a current rent roll, and analyze the market's fundamentals to determine whether the purchase price is appropriate for the property. If other issues are uncovered during the due diligence period, other consultants may be engaged. For example, an inspector may be used to estimate the useful life of a roof so that the fund knows to budget a replacement within the fund's ownership period. Structural consultants may evaluate the property's interior and exterior to determine items for immediate or long-term repair.

When purchasing a multifamily asset, a renovation budget report is conducted. This study explores the estimating of costs to renovate unit interiors and transform common area amenities. A unit renovation budget might contain the expected costs for installing new flooring, windows, lighting, or cabinets, for painting walls, for replacing countertops, or more.

Common area budgets might include the costs to upgrade a pool or clubhouse, remove walls, install new fitness equipment, or replace windows. The fund will receive competitive bids and engage construction management teams early in the process to avoid surprises. The fund's investment management and acquisition teams work cohesively during this process to create and approve a comprehensive renovation budget before submitting an offer for purchase.

Another potential study would be planning for adaptive reuse or development of the property. Properties with vacant land often carry a higher asking price given the added potential for development. Therefore, along with the survey produced as part of the fund's legal due diligence, consultants can assist in determining the potential and cost of any development opportunity. For example, an office building purchased included an adjacent, vacant, one-acre parcel that had a marketed worth of $1 million. A third-party engineering firm determined that to develop the parcel of adjacent land, $750,000 in site costs would be required.

6.3.5. ENVIRONMENTAL DUE DILIGENCE

Environmental remediation can be a significant cost burden,

which is why a fund needs to identify any potential issues prior to closing on the property. An analysis on environmental compliance is done to uncover costly nonconforming uses or conditions that will limit the property's intended use. This cost-benefit analysis is performed during the environmental diligence process to determine whether the project would be feasible. To alleviate the financial burden, municipalities frequently offer incentives to developers through tax breaks.

To determine potential uses during environmental due diligence, a few assessments are conducted. An environmental site assessment is achieved through a preliminary Environmental Site Assessment (ESA), also known as a Phase I report. A Phase I report is completed by a geologist team that determines the historical use of the property and its adjacent parcels and the potential for any environmental contamination from past use. The state of the site and its underlying soil is important, as remediation can be significant and costly if any contamination is present.

Depending on the findings in the Phase I report, a Phase II report might be recommended. The Phase II ESA will include actual soil and groundwater testing to determine if any of the concerns noted in the Phase I report are present. The Phase II will recommend steps to remediate the situation if required.

6.4. UNDERWRITING VARIABLES TO ADD VALUE

During due diligence, how does the investment fund know if the commercial real estate property is worth the investment risk? Will the asset provide a profit and increase in value, or will the asset underperform and lose money? This is the part in the process when underwriting an asset will determine the property's viability and profit potential.

Underwriting a commercial real estate asset is a complex and rigorous process. Hundreds of variables must be analyzed, from the assumed purchase price of a property relative to its competitive set to replacing HVAC to the cost of a fresh coat of paint. All these details can make or break the desired return and have a significant role in the real estate underwriting process.

Any professional private commercial real estate fund will have a rigorous underwriting model to analyze every investment that is a potential acquisition. This ensures consistency and efficiency in the fund's underwriting of assets. It increases the fund's ability to make investments that will meet or exceed the fund's expectations. While a good underwriting process could include dozens of variables, there are five major factors that play a more critical role when analyzing any real estate investment. These are given below.

6.4.1 RENT GROWTH FORECAST

Forecasted rent growth is one of the most important assumptions a real estate investor can make; it's the variable that has compounding effect throughout the duration of the investment. A solid fund should use industry-leading third-party data to assist in projecting rental growth.

Another concept to consider is seasonality. This is more relevant to multifamily properties where most leases are for one year and the demand for new leases peaks between the spring and fall. Seasonality is a function, primarily from life-changing events such as graduation, a new job, marriage, and weather.

Predictability allows fund managers to push rental rates as demand spikes. Given most leases are signed on a twelve-month commitment, it is important to realize what your lease expiration schedule looks like when acquiring a property, as you don't want too many lease expirations occurring in the slow-leasing season of the market. It is also important not to assume all lease expirations occur in the high-demand season, as this can overstate cash flows throughout the asset's holding period.

6.4.2. VACANCY

There are two variables to vacancy: physical vacancy and economic vacancy. Physical vacancy is the actual number of units or square feet that are empty at any given moment. Economic vacancy is the loss of revenue a property will see due to the units undergoing renovations, model or employee units, concessions, or bad debt.

The significance of physical vacancy is critical to understand in every asset class. The best way to forecast it is to look at the submarket level vacancy, comparable assets, and the fund property's historical vacancy. The fund manager should consider the local supply pipeline. Identifying the number of units or square feet coming online from comparable new developments in the near future will play significantly in determining the occupancy and rental rates that can be achieved. Moreover, vacancy loss can be much higher with smaller properties, as each unit or space accounts for a larger share of the property.

Economic vacancy accounts for the physical vacancy, but goes deeper, accounting for loss to lease (units that are leased below market rate), model/employee units, concessions, and bad debt. Most funds will look to reposition assets within a three- to five-year period. During this time period, there will certainly be loss to lease and potential concessions due to improvements made to the asset. It's important to consider the amount of disruption there might be and how it will impact cash flow during the renovation period. Understanding cash flow can lead to budget shortfalls that might require additional equity infusions that could dilute potential returns.

6.4.3. RESETTING TAXES

In most parts of the country, property taxes will most likely be reset based on the property's sale price anywhere between one to three years after the sale transaction occurs. An inaccurate forecast can affect future cash flows and impact exit price substantially, as taxes usually represent anywhere from 15 percent to 45 percent of the property's total operating expenses.

For example, let's assume a property is purchased where taxes are $500,000 for the year 2017. It's estimated that the taxes will increase roughly $100,000 after the property's assessed value is reset. A $100,000 reduction in Net Operating Income (NOI) will reduce the sale price by $2 million at a 5 percent exit cap rate and must be considered prior to formalizing the acquisition price.

6.4.4. EXIT CAP RATE

A capitalization rate, usually referred to as a "cap rate," is the ratio of a property's net operating income (NOI) in the first year of ownership, divided by its purchase price. It's used to determine an appropriate exit cap rate that is used to calculate the gross value of that investment property at sale.

It is important to understand that as the capitalization rate (CAP) increases, the value of the property decreases and vice versa.

A commercial real estate investment fund should factor in the general capital markets in a rising interest rate environment. To determine an exit cap rate, the fund manager should study current cap rates prevailing in the market for properties with similar characteristics. Once it's identified where those cap rates currently stand, the fund manager increases the rate in their calculation by 1–2 percent each year for the duration of the investment's hold period. For example, if a fund purchases a new asset today in a market where comparable properties are currently trading at a 5.0 percent cap rate, the manager would underwrite an exit cap rate at 5.50 percent after year five. Building this cap rate expansion into the underwriting model helps protect the fund from the risk of uncertain market conditions in the future.

6.4.5. DEBT ASSUMPTIONS

A popular choice for private commercial real estate funds is to use floating-rate financing for several reasons, but most importantly because it gives the flexibility to pay off a loan penalty-free when the fund wants to sell the asset. On the other hand, fixed-rate financing often requires borrowers to pay a defeasance fee. Floating-rate debt historically has been less expensive than fixed-rate debt because forecasts of future interest rate hikes usually anticipate greater increases than what actually happens.

Another reason to use floating-rate debt is because funds focus on value-add investments. This type of debt offers a source for future funding to cover some of the additional money needed for capital improvements, and it is generally provided by the same lender who provided the acquisition financing.

While using floating debt, it's important for a fund manager to keep in mind that the rate a borrower pays is based off a forward curve with a spread. Most frequently, the future rate is the one month LIBOR curve. A fund should update their models each week to reflect the most current projections for the curve. When modeling a forward curve, it's important to compute the calculation monthly to avoid underestimating debt payments, as this will result in a lower-than-expected cash flow and net operating income (NOI).

Investors need to understand the assumptions a private commercial real estate fund manager uses in their underwriting model. Even the smallest miscalculation can have serious effects on the returns of an investment. A rigorous underwriting process helps to ensure that an investment will perform as expected and that all opportunities are benchmarked against one another to determine those that represent the best risk-adjusted investments.

6.5. THE VALUE OF TRANSPARENCY

We've covered a lot of information in this chapter regarding due diligence and how to evaluate an investment fund and the assets for your portfolio. An overarching term is a great way to sum it all up, and that is the word "transparent."

In the investment world, both Wall Street and real estate, the words "honesty," "integrity," "client service," "expertise," and "transparency" are all overused. But these words need to be valued and built into the fund's process, documents, and systems rather than just touted out on a website or in marketing materials.

Transparency means providing investors with the information the fund has in real time. Most of the top private commercial real estate funds will have technology and team members that make transparency a part of the way they do business. All of the fund's assets, business plans, and updates should be readily available to any investor. A well-managed fund sends updates every quarter and works within a good communication system. All investors should know what is happening within the fund at all times.

Transparency exists when investors are supplied with all the information they need in an easily available way. Simply conforming to minimum standards of the law should not be the benchmark in a real estate fund in which you'll be investing. All investment fund managers are required by law to disclose conflicts of interest and fees in the prospectus; these are long and tedious documents just like this chapter, with most of the important information buried in the back. This makes it difficult for the investor to see what the fees really are and understand how the fund's distribution works. These tactics cloud the true nature of the costs of investing in vehicles such as non-traded and private REITs. Fees are only one issue, although a significant one: according to the Investment Program Association (IPA), upfront fees associated with investing in a non-traded REIT may be in the range of 12 percent to 15 percent and may involve other fees over the investment's life.[34]

The security of dividends is another clever marketing trick. Most non-traded and private REITs don't have the fund pay all their investors dividends, so their managers entice investors into reinvesting it at a "discount" to share price.

---

34 Ann Marsh, "Commissions Exposed, Advisor Stops Selling Nontraded REITs," *Financial Plannng*, June 8, 2016, https://www.financial-planning.com/news/commissions-exposed-advisor-stops-selling-nontraded-reits.

If the share is $10, but the value of the underlying assets is $3, then reinvesting at $9.50 is like paying a 300 percent premium.

The due diligence process only lasts two to three months, so it's critical the investment team has a process in place. It's an important time in the life cycle of the investment asset, as decisions made during this time can affect the property for many years ahead. By going far beyond standard due diligence procedure, a good fund will set operational priorities that can reduce expenses and speed the pace of value-add improvements.

Keep in mind that if you come across a private commercial real estate fund, and it or its fund manager doesn't meet all the qualifications discussed in this chapter, it should not mean you shouldn't invest. We've discussed an exhaustive list of due diligence materials so the investor will have all the tools necessary to evaluate good private commercial real estate. But do listen for cues in a fund manager's answers that shed light on their honesty and integrity. Does it sound like there is something they're hiding?

So finally, don't commit your hard-earned cash without taking the time to get to know a fund manager on a personal level. Only then can an investor be sure you are investing with true professionals in every sense of the word. It's better to be with a great manager in a good deal than in a great deal with a bad fund manager.

You're probably starting to get a good understanding of why I'm so excited about investing in commercial real estate. But I'm going to warn you, it's only natural you'll come across naysayers. Commercial real estate is often perceived as complex, difficult, and only available to the wealthiest of investors. The naysayers will most often boast of their success in residential real estate and how they know a "guy" who made tons of money with little effort investing in residential real estate. Sure, in rising markets, even the most average person can see an increase in their home or beach house. In the next chapter, we're going to take an honest look into the world of residential real estate investing and why it's not always what you hear at the local barbeque with friends and family.

KEY TAKEAWAYS

- → It can seem a bit adventurous to invest in small private commercial real estate funds. But with the right due diligence, your investment portfolio will thank you time and again.
- → Transparency between the investor and the real estate fund must exist, which means that all the information needed is available in a simple and easy method.
- → It's always a better idea to pick a good fund manager with a good deal, than a great deal with a bad fund manager.
- → Professional fund managers have processes and procedures in place that will share how they conduct their due diligence on assets and underwriting. Make sure you know these, as they indicate the caliber of the manager.
- → Before investing in any fund, investors should make sure that the manager has professional investment documents in place that clearly lay out the investment strategy and business terms of the deal.

CHAPTER 10

RESIDENTIAL REAL ESTATE VS. COMMERCIAL REAL ESTATE INVESTING

"Now one thing I tell everyone is to learn about real estate. Repeat after me, real estate provides the highest returns, the greatest values and the least risk."

—ARMSTRONG WILLIAMS, THE LEADING VOICE FOR AFRICAN AMERICAN INVESTING

Real estate gurus often say, "Residential real estate investing is your path to wealth and riches!" And so you've probably wondered why we haven't talked about investing in residential real estate. Isn't that the best place to invest? So why are we talking about private commercial real estate?

FUN FACT

In Japan, most houses depreciate in value. Half of all houses are demolished within thirty-eight years, and there is virtually no market for preowned homes. Per capita, there are nearly four times as many architects and more than twice as many construction workers in Japan as in the United States.

During the research for this book, I conducted exhaustive searches for real estate investing. The public domain is saturated with articles, educational forums, blogs, etc., on the subject of investing in residential real estate. Why?

10.1. THE MYTH OF RESIDENTIAL REAL ESTATE

The real estate gurus and investing seminar business is a driving factor as to why residential real estate is so popular. *Rich Dad Poor Dad*'s Robert Kiyosaki, Carlton Sheets, Dean Graziosi, Grant Cardone, and *Flipping This House*'s Than Merrill—it's impossible to keep track of these guys and companies in the space as they have a tendency to come and go at a rapid pace.

In 1986, *Money* magazine counted only eighteen real estate investing gurus.[35] Many didn't survive and pivoted to other "get rich quick" schemes. A few survived for the ages, like Robert Allen, who wrote the book *Nothing Down*, and spent

35 "John T. Reed's View of Various Real Estate Investment Gurus," JohntReed.com, September 3, 2015.

over $280 million on television advertising to promote how to build a real estate empire with "nothing down." It's humiliating, but I was even suckered into buying the book and it still sits on my bookshelf.

Then in the 2000s, Robert Kiyosaki arrived and *Rich Dad Poor Dad* became a cult classic. There are over twenty-eight million copies of this book in print all over the world, and you can find it in over fifty languages. Kiyosaki was a struggling Xerox salesman before he cashed in as a guru star; according to the *Wealthy Gorilla*, his empire is now worth over $80 million. His seminars are mostly carnival-style motivational rallies to motivate you to buy his programs.

The reason I mention the guru business is because they've created an army of weekend warriors out to find the next hidden real estate gems. The good news for private commercial real estate investors is they've yet to discover our investment sector.

These guru recruiting events are held all over the country on any given day. The promise to show you the blueprint to build a real estate empire without any money or creating your retirement strategy with buying residential loan notes is just unfair. While there are a few success stories, they are few and far between. Enthusiastic investors attend the seminars, buy the materials, but never really start the hard work required to be successful. Another group of investors will start the process to wealth and identify a property, realize how difficult it is without your personal money, get themselves into a deal where they have no idea what they're doing, and end up losing money and time.

The word "guru" always reminds me of the saying "Those who can, do; those who can't, teach." If the guru were actually successful in making the types of money and returns that they are selling you, wouldn't they be better off not sharing those secrets to anybody who would pay them a couple of thousand dollars? The successful residential home investors have professional systems and processes in place. The inexperienced guru students soon discover this is a business, not a place to invest your hard-earned money.

A friend and colleague was interested in learning how these professional residential investors ran their companies. We only had experience in private commercial real estate. It was our lucky day when the investment team of a successful group reached out to us to create professional business models and pro formas for the residential real estate investment company. It gave us an inside glimpse into what actually happens.

This particular investment group created a portfolio of over twenty-five residential units and was projected to earn almost $200,000 per year in passive income. That certainly got our attention, and I was curious as to how they achieved these returns. The investor provided a list of all the assets, and our firm thoroughly researched the portfolio. After analysis, the facts showed the investor spent nearly $3,000,000 of his personal equity and, over three years, the portfolio of properties only generated about $110,000 in income.

The investor presented his future assumptions and they did report his passive income numbers, but as we dug into them, the assumptions were unrealistic. The investor was assuming his units would be occupied on average 11.5 months per year (4 percent vacancy rate), while historically his units were actually at about an 18 percent vacancy rate. He also assumed he would spend less than $2,000 to turn over each tenant in the future when he was actually spending about $4,000 per new tenant currently.

The biggest fallacy in these assumptions was that he completely ignored any future costs of HVAC, hot water heater, roof replacement, etc., that was certain to happen yearly given the number of units he owned and that the majority of his properties were already twenty-five to thirty-five years old. Using his own historical information as a baseline, we projected a potential annual return from his twenty-five units that was less than $100,000 per year—that's under a 3.5 percent annual return on investment.

One thing I also pointed out to him was that this was far

from a passive investment. He worked a full-time job to make money to help him acquire these properties but spent most of his hours every night and every weekend looking for new properties and overseeing the renovation properties that he had acquired. It was not uncommon for him to be talking with his agent about writing and submitting contracts at 1 a.m. I asked him to think about the number of hours he had spent to make the $100,000 in "passive income" he had made over the previous three years.

We also discovered in our due diligence that seven properties out of the twenty-five-property portfolio were losing money each year. I say this because when I was younger and moving out of a townhouse into a single-family home, I thought it would be a smart investment to just keep my townhouse and rent it out. I won't bore you with all of the details, but in the five years I rented it I never once made money. I was lucky enough to only have two tenants over those five years, never had one late payment, and only had a half month of vacancy total. During the time I rented the townhouse out, the HVAC had to be replaced, a water line under the house busted, a squirrel ate through the exterior near the roof and moved his family in, and they ate through a couple of electrical wires in the attic, etc. I cringed every time my phone rang for those five years just waiting to see what could possibly go wrong next. When I finally sold the townhouse, I celebrated and told myself I would never get sucked into a residential investment again.

Hopefully you get the point. There are so many things that can happen that you cannot plan for, and they make owning one or even a small number of residential units a very risky investment. As the example above shows, even with a relatively large number of units, you may not lose money on the entire portfolio, but your profits are relatively small, the risk is relatively high, and the workload is intense.

If the investor actually makes it through the grind and creates a valid business, the next hurdle is where to keep funding your deals. Attracting capital is extremely difficult, and local community banks will more than likely pass on your venture after financing only a couple of your investments because you become too big a risk to them.

At this point, the investor must seek out hard-money lenders that specialize in residential real estate. The lenders charge serious fees, with significant upfront points and interest rates being charged between 10 percent and 18 percent on a solid deal. The lenders will also require the use of your real estate as collateral.

Another concern with investing in residential real estate is the low barrier to entry. Private commercial real estate is an option that's not suitable for every investor type. In some areas of the country, it's possible to purchase a residential property for as low as $15,000. This fact opens the market to a much greater number of amateur investors and makes it tougher to make a return on investment, because so many investors are willing to overpay to acquire properties. In commercial real estate, where millions of dollars are at stake, the number of investors is significantly less.

There has always been a mystique about commercial real estate: it's complicated, it's hard to understand, it needs large amounts of capital, and so forth. I disagree, and utilizing the method of investing with a quality private real estate fund takes all these misconceptions off the table. But to make things clear, residential and commercial real estate are two completely different assets and need to be treated as such. Financial advisors like to lump the two into one category, but there are significant differences and they should be viewed completely separately as investment options.

One of my best friends was convinced by his financial advisor that his investment portfolio was too heavy in real estate. As a concerned friend, I asked: "What do you mean? I wasn't aware of any private real estate holdings." He said: "I have three townhome investments." Now, he invested in these townhomes with three other friends in a classic syndication. In reality, he only owns a 25 percent position in these investments with his other friends.

This is a perfect example of what we've been speaking to in this book. His Merrill Lynch financial advisor thinks a few investment townhomes with a 25 percent position with his other friends is too heavy. The advisor may not understand the difference between investing in private commercial real estate and townhomes, or his self-interest has influenced his thinking. Any more cash invested in real estate takes away commission dollars for the financial advisor. Not only is the financial advisor misguided in this example, but his client and my friend's investment portfolio also suffers.

10.2. FORCED SAVINGS VS. FORCED APPRECIATION

Let's agree that residential and commercial real estate are two different things.

A stark distinction between the two assets is best described as this: residential real estate is a "forced savings" device, and commercial real estate is a "forced appreciation" tool. The terms of residential real estate as "forced savings" and commercial real estate as a "forced appreciation" are important enough concepts for a full explanation.

Simply put, the real reason residential real estate works in the eyes of most Americans, at least in the financial sense, is the property becomes an automatic savings plan or a "forced savings" plan. But does investing in a home or residential real estate really make sense?

Countless studies prove purchasing residential real estate is an okay average investment. It's not great, but it's not bad either. Most Americans, not being financially savvy, don't agree and think their homes are their investment strategy foundation. These residential investors simply look at what they paid for the asset and the sale price when the asset is sold. The problem with that simple calculation is they've conveniently forgotten about everything from inflation to taxes and maintenance performed on the asset over the years of ownership. It's a scary thought when you begin adding up annual landscaping, the new HVAC system, new roof, painting, and all the renovations required to keep the home fashionably modern.

But there is something special about real estate, a special something that just makes us *want* it. Common sense flies out the window when standing in front of a house; you've got to have it. Have you ever felt that way about buying one hundred shares of Home Depot stock? Probably not.

But the need to own residential real estate is something of a new concept in American history. The University of Pennsylvania professor Thomas Sugrue points out: "Prior to the Great Depression, it was more common to rent a residence than own it."[36] Mortgages were short term, usually three to five years, and the thought of carrying debt was a shameful and embarrassing thing. How times have changed.

36 Eric Hershthal, "The Unmaking of America," *Slate*, November 2, 2015, https://slate.com/culture/2015/11/these-united-states-reviewed-history-of-america-by-glenda-gilmore-and-thomas-sugrue.html.

FUN FACT

Can't find the right property in your market? There's a guy who will sell you an acre of land on the moon for less than $30. I hope his dues are current with the National Realtors Association.

Residential real estate and homeownership today is still championed by the American middle class. Studies show, however, that people in a lower income class and those in higher income classes prefer to rent and not purchase residential real estate. Is there a lesson to be learned?

This was all started by President Franklin D. Roosevelt when he pioneered the thirty-year mortgage.[37] The reason FDR put his agenda forward was the fact that many residential homeowners faced extreme distress in the wake of the Great Depression. The program was instantly a hit and was propelled by returning war veterans after World War II. The G. I. Bill of 1944 offered veterans access to these new thirty-year mortgages with government subsidy as a *thank-you* for defeating the Nazis.[38] War veterans were buying homes as fast as they could build them.

By the year 1950, homeownership surpassed the 50 per-

37 Adriene Hill, "Who Thought 30-Year Mortgages Were a Good Thing?," *Marketplace*, November 25, 2013, https://www.marketplace.org/2013/11/25/who-thought-30-year-mortgages-were-good-thing/.

38 History.com Editors, "G.I. Bill," History.com, June 7, 2019, https://www.history.com/topics/world-war-ii/gi-bill.

cent mark for the first time in American history. In this new way of thinking, having ownership in residential real estate was a status symbol to the middle class and a sure and safe way to build long-term wealth. Sylvia Porter wrote in the *Money Book*: "Taking on regular home mortgage payments becomes a form of 'forced savings' plan in which you build up a long term asset of prime value." Americans believed that if they invested a 20 percent down payment and made their mortgage payments, then over thirty years, a substantial bit of wealth would be waiting for them.

Now you're wondering: *What is "forced appreciation"?*

"Forced appreciation" is the reason why commercial real estate is so exciting and profitable for investors. Most people are familiar with how to place a valuation on a residential property. A realtor will go into the multiple listing database and pull listings that are comparable to your asset. The comparables are the basis to determine the market value of residential properties. There are a few tweaks to comparables, but they determine market value. When determining a valuation on commercial real estate, the comparable method, popular in the world of residential real estate, is not applicable. Whether you realize it or not, this is the Holy Grail of commercial real estate investing.

Professional private commercial real estate managers do not need to guess or create hypotheticals on future property values when using the "forced appreciation" method. It's an impactful investment strategy used in the private commercial real estate arena. When determining a value on a commercial real estate property, it simply comes down to the net operating income (NOI). When a lender or appraiser looks at the property value, they are less concerned about what a neighboring property sold for six months ago; instead, they prefer to determine how much income the property can yield and how much margin to support regular expenses and the amount of margin in income to support the property's debt service (DSCR).

Bear with me—we're going to review a few principles on net operating income and cap rates. To establish the commercial property value, the formula is simple: take the net operating income (NOI) and divide by the cap rate (capitalization rate). The NOI includes all the revenue generated by the property less the operating expenses (not including paying the mortgage). The cap rate is the potential rate of return on the property if it were sold for cash.

To "force appreciate" and increase property value, there are two factors in the equation for investors to understand. One is to increase the NOI, and the other is to decrease the expenses. In most cases, a fund manager can find ways to achieve both, creating a more favorable NOI, which in turn boosts the commercial real estate value significantly. When private commercial real estate fund managers evaluate deals, keeping an eye on the potential for "forced appreciation" is important.

10.2.1. WAYS TO DRIVE "FORCED APPRECIATION"

The number-one way to increase revenue on a property is to increase the rental rate. Let's use a multifamily asset property as an example:

> 15 unit multifamily property = increase the rent by $10 per month
>
> ($10 x 15 units x 12 months) = $1,800 increased NOI

Using a cap rate of 6 percent would result in $1,800/6 percent = increasing the property value of $30,000.

The "forced appreciation" of $30,000 to this property resulted with no additional investment from the investor group. This can't be done in residential real estate. The comps drive the valuation!

Are there other ways to increase NOI besides increasing rental rates? Of course! A few examples:

- Improve units on turnover to obtain better tenants at a higher rental rate.

- Add additional revenue streams: parking fees, on-site laundry, storage lockers.
- Tighten up rent collections, and improve economic occupancy.
- Improve tenant lease renewals by being an exceptional landlord, and provide renewal incentives.
- Renegotiate contract services for better price.
- Institute utility bill back system to transfer back utility costs back to tenants.
- Install energy-efficient items to conserve resources.

Anything the fund manager can do to increase net operating income (NOI) or reduce expenses is going to increase the property value. Let's use these examples to increase NOI with another multifamily case study:

- 200-unit apartment building with an annual NOI of $89,160
- 200unit apartment building: monthly increase per unit/ monthly increased income/annual increased income

By improving the NOI as outlined, the fund manager was able to make the following changes:

- Rent increase: $20/mo/unit = $4,000/mo additional income = $48,000/yr additional income.
- Utility bill back: $15/mo/unit = $3,000/mo additional income = $36,000/yr additional income.

- Renegotiate contracts: $1,500/mo less in expenses = $18,000/yr less in expenses.
- Reduce tenant turnover: $20,000/yr less vacancy and rehab expenses.

Total increase to NOI = $122,000

Using these few examples, the apartment building NOI was increased by $122,000 a year. Let's take a look at what this does to the valuation of the property. The original NOI of the property was $89,160 and adding $122,000 creates a new NOI of $211,160. Applying a cap rate of 6.5 percent:

> Original NOI = $89,160 valuation at 6.5 percent cap rate = $1,371,692
>
> Increased NOI = $211,160 valuation at 6.5 percent cap rate = $3,248,615
>
> A "forced appreciation" = $1,876,923

Increasing the property evaluation by **over $1.8 million** is exciting and quite remarkable, considering how it was done. Could your residential investments or Wall Street portfolio achieve these results?

MIKE'S LAW #10

Forced Appreciation

Great investors like Warren Buffett don't just buy one million shares of Dairy Queen and hope it increases in value. Buffett buys a company with good fundamentals and uses influence to change how the business operates. Not everyone has the purchase power of Buffett; it's not cheap to buy a seat on a company's board of directors.

But commercial real estate presents itself as the ultimate asset to force appreciation.

10.3. RESIDENTIAL REAL ESTATE VS. COMMERCIAL REAL ESTATE

To recap, I've outlined a list of characteristics for both residential and commercial investments.

RESIDENTIAL REAL ESTATE INVESTMENT THINGS TO REMEMBER:

- Average one-year lease terms
- High tenant turnover
- Tenants are transient or don't want to be renters, therefore typically don't take care of the property.
- When a new tenant moves in, a coat of new paint, carpet, or a steam cleaning of carpet is required at a minimum.
- One capital improvement expense will destroy any potential profit and turn an investment to a loss—for example, a new HVAC, fixing a leak in the roof, repairing a water heater that breaks, etc.
- As a landlord, if you hire a property manager, the costs

range from 8 percent to 12 percent of the rent collected plus expenses. Most property managers charge extra to re-lease the property and to manage any significant maintenance and repairs.

- If you don't hire a property manager, you're responsible for leasing the property or will need to hire a real estate agent. You will need to handle all maintenance requests, tenant complaints, and rent collections and will need to factor in your time requirements.
- The renters pay a rental payment, but they do not pay property taxes, condo fees, or homeowner dues. All these extra fees cut into your investment property.
- If you purchase a property for $100,000 with $20,000 cash down and have an NOI of $2,000 after all expenses and debt service, on paper the property will generate a 10 percent cash-on-cash return. But do you know how much a new HVAC system costs? How much it costs to replace a hot water heater? The costs for repair if a squirrel eats a few electrical wires in your roof? In most cases, paying for a few repairs can wash out your profit for a year and quite possibly two to three years.

FUN FACT

Mark Zuckerberg purchased the four houses next to his in Palo Alto and leased them back to the families that lived there. He did it to avoid the houses being marketed as "next door to Mark Zuckerberg."

COMMERCIAL REAL ESTATE THINGS TO REMEMBER:

- Lease terms are typically three to ten or more years.
- Tenant turnover is much lower because moving a business causes serious disruptions on top of the actual expense.
- Common commercial real estate leases have a 3+/- percent per year rental increase, which insulates the property from downturns in the market and even the overall economy.
- Capital reserves are collected and escrowed to handle major capital improvement expenses, and a good fund manager will show that in their projections.
- Property management fees are typically 3 percent to 5 percent of rents collected.

We've covered a lot so far, and I congratulate you for staying with me this long. It's time to bring it all together and discover how I've combined my unique experience in commercial real estate investing and as a financial advisor. I think we all agree at this point: in order to achieve exceptional returns on our investment portfolios, it is critical to employ asset allocation. Next, we're going to see my strategies and solutions to bring about an innovative approach to financial and wealth management.

KEY TAKEAWAYS

- → Don't let the low barrier to entry and guru workshops intrigue you into residential real estate investing. It's a tough game and ultimately a losing proposition for the novice investor.
- → The difference between residential and commercial real estate assets is residential is a "forced saving" device while commercial real estate is a "forced appreciation" tool.
- → Forced appreciation is what makes commercial real estate exciting and profitable for investors.
- → There is very little in common between residential and commercial real estate investing, yet most financial advisors lump them all into the same category.
- → If it were as easy to make money following a guru's advice as they make it seem, why are they so willing to share their secrets for a couple of thousand dollars?

CHAPTER 11

INTEGRATED ASSET MANAGEMENT: A PARADIGM SHIFT IN INVESTING

"If there is any one secret of success, it lies in the ability to get the other person's point of view and see things from that person's angle as well as from your own."

—HENRY FORD

Future economic forecasts are warning of turbulent times... Business cycles are natural, and that's not going to change. As investors, it's our responsibility to take back control of our money. High stock market returns are not going to last forever. Even corporate earnings are being lowered by economists.

My unique perspective of being an active investor in commercial real estate and a financial advisor puts me in the perfect place to provide guidance on how to build a solid performing investment portfolio. After considerable research on investment strategy, the evidence speaks for itself: asset allocation is the most critical decision you'll make as an investor. You've heard the saying "Don't put all your eggs in one basket." Diversification is the only way to go.

11.1. INTEGRATED ASSET MANAGEMENT

Here's what I've found: true diversification can be achieved through an Integrated Asset Management model.

Let's compare the numbers of a traditional Wall Street investment portfolio versus a private commercial real estate portfolio over the last twenty years between 1999 and 2018.

Between 1999 and 2018:

	MARKET RATE OF RETURN	INITIAL INVESTMENT	TOTAL INVESTMENT RETURN
S&P 500	2.74 percent IRR	$100,000	$167,126
Private Real Estate (CRE)	11.2 percent IRR	$100,000	$750,000

Now let's combine commercial real estate and a traditional Wall Street portfolio through an Integrated Asset Management model. Take a look at the results below.

This is an integrated portfolio with 75 percent stocks and 25 percent private commercial real estate, which is recommended for high-net-worth investors with a net worth of $3 million and below:

RATE OF RETURN	INITIAL INVESTMENT	TOTAL INVESTMENT RETURN	ROI
6.19 percent IRR	$100,000	$312,844	212.8 percent

The returns are even more remarkable with an integrated portfolio with 54 percent stocks and 46 percent private commercial real estate, which is recommended for individuals with a net worth over $10 million on average:

RATE OF RETURN	INITIAL INVESTMENT	TOTAL INVESTMENT RETURN	ROI
8.05 percent IRR	$100,000	$435,247	335.2 percent

The results show that by using simple asset allocation with the addition of private commercial real estate, the investment portfolio increases the overall returns significantly the more you allocate into private commercial real estate. *This is how the rich really do get richer*. The wealthiest investors will invest the same $100,000 as the average investor, but at the end of twenty years, the average investor, investing all in mutual funds with his financial advisor, ends up making $67,126 off of his money, while the wealthiest investors make $335,247 off of that same $100,000.

This is the secret the uber-rich know and understand.

Can you imagine if you allocated more money into private commercial real estate? And you don't even need to be uber-rich to implement these techniques.

The Integrated Asset Management model above was created with a conservative allocation of private commercial real estate. *Bloomberg* reports that out of $51 billion in assets held by high-net-worth individuals, the individual investor held on average around 33 percent of their portfolios in private commercial real estate.[39] The Urdang Securities Management study by Stephen Lee, of the Cass Business School in London, concluded: "Optimally investors would include 26 percent allocation to private real estate."[40]

The precise asset allocation always comes down to personal preference and investment criteria for the individual investor. This should be determined with the expertise of your financial advisor and real estate professionals. Family

39 Michael Episcope, "Six Reasons Private Equity Real Estate Funds Are an Attractive Alternative to Private REITS," *Forbes*, November 9, 2017, https://www.forbes.com/sites/forbesrealestatecouncil/2017/11/09/six-reasons-private-equity-real-estate-funds-are-an-attractive-alternative-to-private-reits/#88393a064a95.

40 Ian Ippolito, "How Much Real Estate Should I Have in My Portfolio," *The Real-Estate Crowdfunding Review*, January 10, 2018, https://www.therealestatecrowdfundingreview.com/how-much-real-estate-is-ideal-for-my-por.

offices, endowments, and ultra-high-net-worth individuals routinely place as much as 50 percent of their portfolios in private commercial real estate.

Harry Markowitz, the Nobel Prize-winning father of modern portfolio theory says it best: "Diversification is the only free lunch." Investing your money across different asset classes for true asset allocation decreases your risk, increases your upside returns over time, and doesn't cost you anything.

My grandfather taught me from an early age not to put all my eggs in one basket. You've heard the same adage for years. The sad truth is that sophisticated investors have been putting all their eggs in one basket and were not even aware they were doing so, most likely through mutual funds and managed equity portfolios. Your "eggs" need to be placed across different asset classes for true diversification. Having your money diversified among stocks and bonds doesn't give you the benefit once expected. Only by tearing down the inherent conflict of interest between financial advisors and private real estate can investors enjoy the benefits of diversification.

An integrated investment portfolio will produce incredible returns only possible with this innovative practice of combining expertise that will give investors peace of mind regardless of the economic climate.

"Wide diversification is only needed when investors don't understand what they're doing."

—WARREN BUFFETT

11.2. INTEGRATED ASSET MANAGEMENT IS A LEADER'S CHOICE

Ray Dalio, a billionaire investor and hedge fund manager, explained asset allocation as the only way to ensure survival and success. "Owning 15 uncorrelated investments, you can reduce your overall risk by about 80 percent, and you'll increase the return to risk ratio by a factor of five. So your return is five times greater by reducing risk." Dalio built his investment portfolio around stocks, bonds, gold, commodities, real estate, and other alternatives.

A leader in modern-day portfolio management theory is the chief investment officer of Yale University's endowment, David Swensen. Swensen utilizes both public and private investments to give the endowment portfolio the best results possible. He grew the fund from $1 billion to over $23.9 billion with annual returns of 13.9 percent over thirty years. What's his secret?

There are three rules of investing according to Swensen. These rules will reduce your risk and increase your returns.

1. Security selection: Picking the right equities.

2. Market timing: Getting in and out of markets.
3. Asset allocation: Long-term strategy with diversified investments.

According to Swensen: "Overwhelmingly, the most important of the three is asset allocation. It actually explains more than a hundred percent returns in the investment world."

Investors must follow the principle of diversification as a core foundation for long-term financial success. Making intelligent decisions allocating your investment strategy will put you in the top 1 percent of all investors. It's the choice leaders make.

11.3. MAKING INTEGRATED ASSET MANAGEMENT A REALITY

It's time for financial advisors and private commercial real estate professionals to work together for the best interest of the client. This is an easy statement to make in theory. But what if it could really happen? Some seemingly impossible things in life can be clarified with simple elegance. Could an Integrated Asset Management approach become this simple elegance? And how do we make it a reality?

Recent studies show that 60 percent of high-net-worth investors plan on decreasing their position in the stock market in search of better opportunities. Moreover, 90 percent of high-net-worth investors surveyed have invested in private commercial real estate opportunities without any help from their financial advisor.[41]

But what I just said is a double-edged sword. Of the high-net-worth individuals who were advised by their financial advisors on private commercial real estate, the opportunities discussed were simply not the best choices. Financial advisors do what they know best: tell investors to pick REITs and large real estate funds like Blackstone and Starwood. Now we all know this is a great strategy if you're looking for average or below-average returns. We also know the big companies like JPMorgan, Merrill Lynch, Goldman Sachs, and Morgan Stanley would never show a client small private commercial real estate. Why? Financial advisors don't understand this investment opportunity, their companies don't provide the investments, and most important—it doesn't make their companies money!

We know how the big Wall Street firms operate, but what about the smaller, independent wealth firms? In earlier chapters I've placed the big wirehouse brokerage companies on the firing line. Could it be possible that smaller, independent registered investment advisors (RIA) provide these real estate options to their clients? Maybe that's the answer or maybe not!

---

41 Yun Li, "More Than Half of World's Richest Investors See a Big Market Drop in 2020," CNBC, November 12, 2019, https://www.cnbc.com/2019/11/12/more-than-half-of-the-richest-investors-see-a-big-market-drop-in-2020.html.

MIKE'S LAW #11

Leadership Mentality

Followers don't make good investment advisors.

Today's financial advisors are discouraged from making independent investment decisions. Instead, they are glorified salespeople trained to sell you investment products that make their companies the most profit—otherwise known as "followers." In reality, financial advisors are punished for thinking original thoughts. Wirehouse brokerage firms like Merrill Lynch, Morgan Stanley, and Goldman Sachs will not allow their financial advisors to discuss these investment products, because it takes money out of their pockets.

Leadership is thinking for oneself and inspiring vision to create new opportunities. "Leadership is the capacity to translate vision into reality," according to Warren Bennis. As an investor, make sure you look for a leader as your financial advisor—someone who is not afraid to think out of the box and develop innovative investment strategies. It will prove to be a wise investment decision. Moreover, cultivate a leadership mentality yourself so that you can recognize which advisors to trust and which ones to steer clear of, as well as which ideas are good and which to avoid.

An independent investment firm by the name of Creative Planning is getting a lot of attention these days. According to their website, Barron's names them the "No. 1 Independent Wealth Management Firm in America" and they are CNBC's "No. 1 Independent Wealth Management Firm in America."

The company proudly boasts what makes them different:

"We do not offer proprietary mutual funds or hedge funds,

thus avoiding significant conflict of interest. We only select investment vehicles from the available universe of securities considered best in class for our clients' needs, so our compensation is the same regardless of which investments we recommend."

Nothing innovative, they're just selling the same fee-heavy mutual funds everyone else sells. I also beg to differ: there *is* a "conflict of interest."

"Our investment portfolio recommendations are tailored to your personal situation. We will be there to guide you in selecting the right asset allocation and investment strategy for your needs. Our goal is to help you not only make the right decisions in the short term but also help you realize your long-term goals."

I don't mean to pick on Creative Planning, but come on, is this what they call innovating the financial service industry? Are they really providing the "right asset allocation"? The answer is no. They actually say, "We exist because the financial advising industry is broken. We believe our service should be completely in your best interest, not ours. We can't change Wall Street, but we can offer something different to like-minded investors." Now we agree on something: "the financial advising industry is broken." But what's different in their strategy? Not a damn thing...

So what can an investor do?

Let's go back to the beginning of the book. What would the great innovator Henry Ford do on such an occasion? Innovation and fresh ideas are seriously in need for the financial service business, and we certainly don't need "faster horses." We need better advisors.

In researching for this book, I've looked all over the place for new ideas, led conversations with leaders in financial management, and interviewed alternative investment professionals, which included commercial real estate experts. I'll be honest: I'm a bit frustrated and angry over this. But there is an opportunity in every crisis, and the deeper the crisis, the better the opportunity. The fractured mindset in today's financial management industry is nothing more than a crisis. How do we bring the experts together? The financial advisors, real estate experts, and accounting and legal services.

A new way of doing business is upon us.

We've proven Integrated Asset Management is the answer, but how do we make it happen? Put financial advisors and real estate experts in the same company. Eliminate the conflict of interest and put the client's interest first. No longer would the financial advisor and real estate professional be compensated in relation to their particular investments and advice.

Throughout history, we've seen effective partnerships move business leaders to achieve more and bring better products to the market. There are many examples of these business partnerships. Steve Jobs knew his Apple processors were not best in class. Jobs couldn't move forward with his groundbreaking vision without the best processors. He just couldn't get his team to catch up to the leading processor company, namely Intel. And so he partnered with them. If the superego of Steve Jobs can create a partnership with Intel to propel his company to create some of the best technology products ever imagined, can the financial advisory world create a partnership with commercial real estate professionals to give their clients superior returns on investment?

Not only is this possible...we've made it a priority.

"The secret to golf is to turn three shots into two."

—BOBBY JONES

This investment advisory approach is a solution to cure the blind spot in wealth management tied to real estate assets.

In today's financial planning industry, investors rely on their financial advisor to make investment choices. We've proven asset allocation is the most important decision for investors to make within their portfolios. If the typical financial advisor has no knowledge or ability to recommend private real estate investment opportunities, what should an investor do?

Before the creation of Integrated Asset Management, investors needed to be proactive in search of private commercial real estate investments. It's not easy—I'm not sure where you would start. One recommendation would be networking with an attorney, banker, and CPA professional for recommendations. The innovative approach to financial planning is upon us and will give investors the advice required for intelligent investment planning.

Integrated Asset Management incorporates real estate asset planning into traditional investment portfolio management to provide investors with honest asset allocation. True asset allocation is how investors drive returns in a safe and consistent manner.

We've learned investors require both the financial advisor and real estate expert to help them manage their assets in proper fashion. Getting these two advisors to agree on how assets should be allocated, which risks are appropriate, and how to achieve the same financial goal is unrealistic. This is a real dilemma facing investors every day. Integrated Asset Management can innovate and solve the problem for investors.

Industries change all the time. Integrated Asset Management is following in the footsteps of many industries that have been shaped to provide a better service for their customers. For example, the movie rental business. Back in the day, Blockbuster was the dominant player in movie rentals. It was a real treat to visit your local Blockbuster store and roam the aisles for your weekend movie choice. Just remember to rewind before you return!

In 2002, a vending company by the name of Red Box entered the scene and offered movie rentals in vending machines. You've probably seen them at your grocery store and other places around town. Then Netflix went one step further and allowed its customers to order movies through a mail-order service. You could order a bunch of movies and mail them back at your discretion. With the technology advancements of online streaming, Netflix smartly pivoted to become the leader in video streaming and changed the industry forever. Netflix is now the seventh-largest internet company in the world.

Each step of the way, the industry changed and old business models were phased out. Today, the financial service industry is demanding more expertise from its financial advisors. Discovering a financial advisor willing to implement the Integrated Asset Allocation is critical for your ability to build generational wealth and peace of mind. In the following conclusion, you'll see exactly how to find this type of advisor and take back control of your investment portfolio.

KEY TAKEAWAYS

- → Asset allocation is the most critical decision you'll make as an investor.
- → Asset allocation means more than diversification. You must divide your assets among different asset classes, such as stocks, bonds, and private real estate investments.
- → Most financial advisors' definition of asset allocation and the true definition of asset allocation used by high-net-worth individuals and family offices are not even close to the same.
- → Average high-net-worth investors have about 33 percent of their money invested in real estate.
- → Sixty percent of high-net-worth individuals are planning to decrease their stock portfolio in search of better opportunities.
- → Combining financial advisors with private real estate experts is the next innovative way of future financial planning.

CONCLUSION

It's true. The rich do get richer. And it's also true that wealth inequality is a big and growing problem in the United States. Over these pages, we've learned that wealth creation is not simply a debate over inequality, government involvement, or tax treatment. The wealthy become wealthy and increase their wealth because of better asset allocation in their investment portfolios.

In contrast, the middle class remain stagnant in wealth because of bad investing. The middle class had 63 percent of their assets invested in their homes. The wealthiest investors invest over three-quarters of their assets into investments, mostly businesses and private commercial real estate. Edward Wolff, an economist at New York University, found that the wealth gap has increased sharply from 2007 to today.[42] His study found the wealthy invested

42 Robert Frank, "It's True, the Rich Do Get Richer—Here's Why," CNBC, November 18, 2014, https://www.cnbc.com/2014/11/18/heres-why-the-rich-do-get-richer.html.

heavily in high-performing assets with average annual returns of 5.91 percent versus a meek 3.27 percent earned by the middle class. He also noted that during the Great Recession years, the middle class were busy selling investments to pay down debts, while the wealthy were growing and maintaining their investments.

The strategies and concepts we've discussed can easily be implemented in your investment life, and this is critical to your future's wealth. We cannot expect exceptional investment returns consistently over time by using what the Wall Street marketing machine and our traditional financial advisor tell us.

It's your decision. Do you want your money working at its highest capacity? Right now, high-net-worth individuals are including commercial real estate investments 46 percent or more of the time than the average investor.[43] As we saw in the last chapter, an integrated portfolio between 1999 and 2018 realized over 335 percent return on investment, as opposed to a traditional Wall Street portfolio. Don't jeopardize your financial future by listening to the counsel of traditional Wall Street financial advisors. The rich get richer by thinking independently.

---

43 M. Szmigiera, "Investments of High Net Worth Individuals- Statistics and Facts," *Statista*, November 12, 2019, https://www.statista.com/topics/2701/investments-of-high-net-worth-individuals/.

My personal journey gave me the unique perspective to tell this story. Years of experience, study, and frustration opened my eyes to a new approach.

Investment diversification and proper asset allocation will make this happen for you as well. All investment portfolios must have proper division among different asset classes. We are often misinformed by financial advisors that asset allocation is simply defined as diversification. Real diversification is not placing a mix of stocks and bonds. The best-performing investment portfolios have long-term allocation strategies in other asset classes that don't involve Wall Street. Your investment portfolio should include real estate, commodities, along with stocks and bonds.

As Henry Ford expressed so eloquently: "If I had asked people what they wanted, they would have said faster horses." Today's investors really aren't privy to the knowledge discussed in these pages. So how on Earth would investors know their available options to make informed decisions? Our investment lives need innovation and new ideas. I certainly hope this book has piqued your interest in learning more about different investing techniques. When the bear market returns from hibernation, I hope you're prepared and not still relying on advice from conforming Wall Street advisors.

The time to act is now. Here are a few steps every smart investor should take:

1. Take personal responsibility and control of your investment and financial life. You cannot rely on your financial advisor as your only source for information and advice. Oftentimes, as we've learned, financial advisors may have good intentions, but do not provide or have the knowledge of alternative investments not correlated to Wall Street.
2. Don't be afraid to question your financial advisor. Challenge your advisors on alternative investing, and be wary of "big brand" funds they may offer, which are often not really alternatives, but simply bloated Wall Street funds disguised as alternative investments.
3. Don't be afraid to look at other investment opportunities on your own. Do your own research and talk with other investors and read alternative investment materials.
4. Nobody is going to deliver these investment opportunities on your doorstep. Oftentimes, a traditional financial advisor cannot and will not provide alternative investments, especially private commercial real estate. Beware of the real estate investment REIT discussion. These are basically stock funds correlated to Wall Street.
5. Don't hesitate or allow fear to creep in when your traditional Wall Street financial advisor tells you to stay away from these investment techniques. Remember, you're

taking money out of their pockets. Only you have your best interests in mind.

6. Find trustworthy advisors to assist you in proper due diligence before entering into any new investment opportunity. If necessary, consult with your CPA and attorney before entering into any new investment opportunities.
7. If you want to make these exceptional returns like the ultra-wealthy, you're going to need to ultimately trust this new way of thinking and trust new partnerships. Some alternative investments will allow minimum investment as low as $25,000. This will give you a low-risk opportunity to become comfortable.
8. Sign up for educational newsletters, podcasts, and other informative sites that provide current alternative investing information and opportunities. Search online with a few common search words such as "private commercial real estate investing," "passive income," and "alternative investing" to locate research materials.
9. Locate a financial advisor who understands the concepts of Integrated Asset Allocation and discuss your personal investment portfolio. If you can locate a financial advisor who understands the concepts of this book, you've made a connection that will serve you well. They do exist, so network to locate and start a conversation.
10. Research private commercial real estate professionals in your area and reach out for a personal meeting. Search for private real estate fund managers and real estate investment companies.

We've covered a lot of material in this book. My purpose was to open your eyes to how Wall Street works and how traditional financial advisors should not be the only professionals guiding you through the complex world of investments. All investors need the fundamental service of an Integrated Asset Allocation financial advisor.

I hope you've enjoyed learning about my investment philosophy of integrating commercial real estate within your investment portfolio. For more information on my personal commercial real estate investment fund, you may visit our website at www.RedFoxCapital.CO and join our newsletter and receive free investment articles we periodically send our clients. In addition, if you would like more information on Integrated Asset Management and how to professionally create an integrated investment portfolio, please email me directly at my personal address mbrown@redfoxcommercialllc.com, and visit my dedicated website at www.generationalprivatewealth.com. It's my personal duty to help investors to learn more about Integrated Asset Management and the easy steps to implementing such a financial plan. I will give you an easy blueprint on next steps and how to evaluate advisors.

I've also included a free bonus chapter download on www.generationalprivatewealth.com to determine if you are working with the right financial advisor to achieve the successful investing results we've discussed in this book. Read through the chapter and maintain an open mind... It may be necessary to make a change.

Thank you and happy investing!

GLOSSARY

Abatement. (1) A reduction in the property tax bill, usually a result of successfully contesting the assessed value. (2) A reduction of environmental contamination. (3) A reduction in rent.

Absorption rate. The rate at which vacant space is filled, or units in a building or lots in a subdivision are sold. This is a way of calculating demand.

Acceleration clause. Clause used in a note and mortgage (or deed of trust) that gives the lender the right to demand payment in full after a default by the borrower.

Accessibility. The ease of access to a site by customers, employees, carriers, and others necessary to the intended use of the property. To be "handicapped accessible" involves compliance with various federal, state, and local codes.

Accrued interest. Interest on a debt instrument that has been earned but not yet paid. Since interest is usually paid in arrears, accrued interest may not necessarily indicate a delinquency in payment.

Acquisition costs. Total costs of acquiring a property, including amounts paid to seller and other related costs and fees.

Acre. A measure equal to 43,560 square feet or 160 square rods configured in any shape. It usually refers to land.

Ad valorem. "According to value." A method of taxation using the value of the item taxed to determine the amount of tax. Taxes can be either "ad valorem" or "specific." For example, a tax of $5.00 per $10,000 of value per property is "ad valorem." A tax of $5.00 per property is "specific."

Addition. A portion of a building added to the original structure.

Adjustable mortgage loans (AMLS). Mortgage loans under which the interest rate is recalculated periodically based on a predetermined formula—such as in relation to changes in the Treasury rate for thirty-year bonds—to more closely coincide with current rates. AMLS are also called adjustable rate loans, adjustable rate mortgages (ARMS), flexible rate loans, or variable rate loans.

Adjusted funds from operations (AFFO). A performance measure used to analyze REITs. AFFO is intended to provide a better approximation of REIT cash flow than funds from operations (FFO, see below). AFFO is a refinement of FFO that is calculated by starting at FFO and subtracting a reserve for normal capital expenditures as well as leasing and tenant improvements.

Agent. One who is authorized to act for or represent another, usually in business matters. The agent's authority may be express or implied.

Air rights. The right to the use of the air space above the property without the right to use the surface of the property. Such air rights may restrict the surface rights of the owner of the land.

Amortization of loan. Repayment of debt through installments of principal payments.

Amortization schedule. A schedule specifying loan payments to be applied to reduction of the principal balance. Most loans call for a constant monthly payment of interest and principal where the portion allocable to principal increases as the balance of the loan and the interest needed to service the loan decreases.

Amortization term. The time period over which the principal amount would be retired on the basis of periodic installments specified to be paid. Not to be confused with the mortgage term (see below).

Anchor tenants. The largest tenants in a shopping center, usually the department stores. The strength of the anchor tenants greatly affects the rentability of the smaller stores and the availability of financing for the shopping center. The term may also be used to describe a major tenant in an office building, industrial park, etc.

Appraisal. An opinion of value based upon a factual analysis by a disinterested person of suitable qualifications.

Appraisal methods. In an appraisal, the valuation is usually based on three major methods: cost approach, income approach, or market value (comparables) approach.

Appraiser. An individual who has the experience, training, and legal qualifications to appraise or value real or personal property. Appraisers must be certified or licensed by the state in order to appraise property involving a federally insured or regulated agency.

"As is" condition. The condition of the property existing at the time of the sale or the signing of a lease for occupancy of a particular space. An "as is" clause is used to limit the warranty of the lessor or seller. Also referred to as an "as is where is" clause.

Assemblage. The acquisition of contiguous properties into one ownership for a specific use.

Assessed value. Value placed upon a property for real estate tax purposes by the local tax assessors, generally broken down between land and building values.

Assignment of lease. The transfer by a lessee to a third party of the exact interest of said lessee. It differs from and should not be confused with a sublease. Assignment and/or subleasing may be restricted in the lease.

Assumption of mortgage. Agreement by a buyer to assume the liability under an existing note secured by a mortgage or deed of trust. The lender usually must approve the new buyer. The existing debtors may or may not be released from their liability.

Basis for depreciation. The value of property for purposes of depreciation. Generally, the property's basis is calculated by adding the total costs of acquisition and the costs of capital improvement less the value of the land.

Blanket mortgage. (1) A mortgage covering more than one property of the mortgagor, such as a mortgage covering all the lots of a builder in a subdivision. (2) A mortgage covering all real property of the mortgagor.

Blueprint. A plan of a building in such detail as to enable contractors to build or remodel space. The name comes from the photographic process that produces the plan in white on a blue background.

Bridge or gap financing. A form of interim loan made to cover a temporary cash shortfall.

Build to suit. A method of constructing property whereby the contractor customizes the building to the user's specifications, often at a previously agreed-to price or rental.

Building code. A comprehensive set of the state or municipal laws that control the construction or remodeling of buildings, including design, materials used, and construction methods.

Capitalization rate. Also known as "cap rate." A rate of return used to calculate the capital value of an unlevered income stream. In a way, it is the inverse of a price/earnings ratio. The formula is value equals the net operating income divided by the cap rate. Because the cap rate is applied to only one year of income, it is often referred to as the "current expected yield before capital expenditures." The income stream may be based on the current, prior, or stabilized year.

Carrying charges. (1) The costs of owning a property that has not yet reached positive cash flow. (2) The financing costs of a property.

Cash flow after financing. Equal to cash flow from operations (see below) less any financing charges such as interest and principal payments or any ground lease payments.

Cash flow from operations. Net operating income (see below) less an allowance for normal capital expenditures and leasing costs.

C-Corporation. The standard legal form of corporate entity, in which all shareholders own stock in the company and have liability limited to their invested capital. Profits in C-corporation are taxed at the corporate level, which is not the case with profits in a Subchapter S-corporation (see below). In addition, shareholders are subject to taxation on dividends from the corporation.

Certificate of occupancy. A certificate issued by a local building department stating that the building has met all applicable codes and is in proper condition to be occupied.

Closed-end fund. A fund that does not accept new investors. The shares generally are not sold and redeemed through the fund but on the open market. The fund may have a limited offering time frame and a predetermined life span.

Closing statement. The statement that lists details of the financial settlement between buyer and seller. Costs include not only the transfer price of the property, but also such items as transfer taxes, recording costs, title insurance, allocated operating expenses including property taxes, and other payments or fees due at the closing such as to third-party brokers.

Cluster zoning. Zoning allowing the construction of building closer together than otherwise permitted under the zoning code. As compensation the balance of the property is kept as open space, often under common ownership.

Commercial mortgage-backed securities (CMBS). A group of mortgages that are packaged together and sold as bonds. The mortgage packages may be broken up into tranches of varying durations and risks. Investors are able to diversify the geographic and property-type risk as well as obtain greater liquidity.

Commingled fund. Also known as "pooled fund." A real estate mutual fund in which the investments of multiple investors are lumped together and generally invested in a variety of properties, in either open-end funds (see below) or closed-end funds.

Common area. For lease purposes, the areas of land and building that are available for the nonexclusive use of all its tenants—e.g., lobbies, corridors, parking lots.

Common area maintenance (CAM). Office, retail, and warehouse tenants and condominium owners often pay, on a proportionate basis, CAM charges, through which they collectively reimburse the landlord for certain agreed-upon expenses that relate to such items as maintenance, servicing of common areas, management, and in the case of retail centers, advertising and promotion.

Condominium property. A structure of two or more units in which the interior space of each unit is individually owned and the balance of the property (both land and building) is owned in common by the owners of the individual units. The size of each unit is measured from the interior surfaces (excluding of paint or other finishes) of the exterior walls, floors, and ceiling. The balance of the property is called the common area and generally is collectively maintained through CAM charges assessed to unit owners.

Cooperative property. A structure of two or more spaces in which the right to occupy a defined space is given in return for the purchase of stock in a corporation that owns the property. Shareholders also agree to pay their share of the common expenses of the property.

Cost of occupancy. The total cost to occupy a property. Such costs include not only basic rent, but additional charges paid to the landlord or paid directly by the tenant for such items as utilities, property taxes, insurance, cleaning, and maintenance including real estate taxes.

Cost plus contract. A building contract setting the builder's profit at a set percentage of the actual cost of labor, materials, and an agreed-upon overhead.

Current yield. A measurement of investment returns based on the percentage relationship of current, annual cash income to the actual cost or the current value of the property.

Custom builder. One who builds for a specific owner, designing the building in advance to suit said owner's need, rather than building for outside sale.

Dark store clause. A clause usually found in retail store leases stating that the tenant must stay open for business.

Debt or loan constant. The percentage relationship of the annual financing payments of interest and principal to the initial face amount of the loan. For example, a $ 1,000 loan at 9 percent interest repaid over a twenty-year period has a constant payment of 10.8 percent.

Deed in lieu of foreclosure. A deed given by an owner/

borrower to a lender to prevent the lender from bringing foreclosure proceedings on the property being held as a security.

Depreciable life. The number of years over which an asset is depreciated, either for income tax purposes or for financial reporting purposes.

Depreciable property. Property for which a useful life can be determined for depreciation purposes. For example, a building and its improvements are depreciable, but the land under it is not, as it is deemed to have an unlimited life.

Depreciation. (1) Decrease in value to real property improvements caused by physical, economic, or functional deterioration or obsolescence. (2) A loss in value expressed as a deduction for income tax or financial statement purposes.

Direct reduction mortgage. A mortgage on which the level of principal payments stays constant, with interest being computed on the remaining balance. The amount of the total payment declines as the principal balance of the mortgage is reduced.

Due diligence. The process of underwriting a property by a prospective buyer or lender prior to the legal closing of a transaction. It encompasses a wide range of activities ranging from physical and environmental inspections, to verifying the validity of leases, to examining the legal title to the property.

Easement. The right, privilege, or interest that one party has in the land of another, such as for a utility line to pass through a property.

EBITDA. Earnings before interest, taxes, depreciation, and amortization. It is often used in measuring the performance of a public company.

Eminent domain. The right of the government or a public utility to acquire property for necessary public use by condemnation. The owner must be fairly compensated.

Enterprise or franchise value. The perceived ability of a management team to add value and generate growth in funds from operations (see below). Used often in valuating real estate investment trusts (see below).

Environmental impact report (EIR). A report of the probable environmental effects of a development on the site and its surrounding area, looking at such features as air quality, traffic, volume, and soil erosion. It also evaluates the proposed building's compliance with certain environmental standards and regulations as well as the existing soil and building conditions. The report is prepared by an independent company to guidelines set by regulators, lenders, or potential purchasers. A Phase I report primarily reviews the history of and title to the site and involves a visual inspection whereas a Phase II assessment involves more physical testing of the soil.

Equity. (1) Any ownership investment (stocks, real estate, etc.) as opposed to an investment in a debt instrument. (2) The market value of real property, less the amount of existing liens. (3) A legal doctrine based on fairness, rather than strict interpretation of the letter of the law.

ERISA. The employee retirement income security act is a law that governs the operation of most private pension and benefit plans. The act established guidelines for the management of pension fund assets and stimulated investment in areas such as real estate for diversification purposes.

Escalation clause. A clause in a lease providing for an increased rental at a future time based on (1) a predetermined amount, (2) a cost of living adjustment using a particular index, (3) an increase in prescribed expenses.

Estoppel. A doctrine of law that stops one from later denying facts that were once acknowledged to be true and others accepted on good faith. Estoppel agreements confirming existing lease terms and specifying any current defaults under the lease are often obtained from existing tenants prior to a new owner's taking possession of a property or prior to a new loan's being put on record. The procedure for obtaining the estoppel agreement is spelled out in the lease.

Fair market value. The price that would likely be negotiated between a willing seller and a willing buyer in an arm's length or independent transaction over a reasonable time frame.

Financial leverage. Given the use of debt in a capital structure, the resulting financial leverage can be either positive or negative. For example, if the cost of the debt—i.e., the principal and interest payment—is 8 percent and the return on assets is 10 percent, an increase in the amount of the loan will increase the return on assets. Conversely, if the debt constant is 11 percent, an increase in debt will result in negative leverage.

Financing costs. Debt or mortgage payments of principal and interest, often in the form of a constant payment that amortizes the loan over a given time period.

First refusal right. The right to match an existing offer either to lease or to purchase an existing property usually within a specified time frame.

Floor area ratio (FAR). The ratio obtained by dividing the gross floor area of all buildings located upon a lot or parcel of land by the total area of the lot or parcel. Zoning ordinances regularly prescribe maximum allowable floor area ratios, as well as height restrictions. Depending on local rules, some square footage, such as space used for underground parking, may be excluded in calculating floor area.

Foreclosure sale. A sale of property used as security for a debt, to satisfy a default. Sale is often at public auction.

Frontage. The linear measurement along the front of a parcel or space, or in some cases along the side abutting a waterway or walkway.

Full disclosure. In real estate, revealing all the known facts that may affect the decision of a buyer or tenant.

Funds from operations (FFO). A performance measure used to analyze REITs. FFO is determined by starting with net income, adding back real estate related depreciation and amortization, and then deducting for nonrecurring items, such as gains or losses on asset sales. REIT prices are often described and compared in terms of an FFO multiple, which is the ratio of price to FFO.

General partner. In a partnership, the partner who conducts the business and whose liability is not limited. All partners in an ordinary partnership are general partners. A limited partnership must have at least one general partner, which may be an individual or a corporation.

Grandfather clause. The clause in a law permitting the continuation of a use, business, etc., that, when established, was permissible but, because of a change in the law, is now not permissible.

Gross area. The entire physical area of all floor space in a parcel of land or in a building, often measured in square feet or square meters.

Gross lease. A lease that obligates the lessor to pay all or part of the operating expenses of the leased property, such as real estate taxes, insurance, maintenance, and utilities as well as the base rent.

Ground lease. A lease of land, or land exclusive of the building on it, usually obtained so that the lessor can develop a building or otherwise generate cash from the site. It is usually written as a net lease with the lessee paying all expenses.

Ground rent. Rent paid for vacant land. If the property is improved, ground rent is that portion attributable to the land only, although the amount of the payment may reflect the value of the building on it.

Hard costs. Development costs for tangible improvements, such as roads and sidewalks, shell construction, finish-out of units and landscaping.

Highest and best use. The use of land under its current legal strictures that will produce the highest economic value and that is legally, physically, and financially feasible.

Holdover tenant. A tenant who retains possession after the expiration of a lease.

Holdback. Portion of a loan or payment held back until a contingency is met.

Housing starts. Number of homes or units on which construction has begun. The figures are used to determine the availability of housing, the need for real estate loans, the need for labor and materials, etc.

HVAC. Heating, ventilating, and air conditioning system.

Institutional lenders. Banks, insurance companies, pension funds, and other similar businesses that make loans to the public in the ordinary course of business.

Internal rate of return (IRR). The discount rate at which the present value of the future cash flows of an investment equals the cost of the investment. It is used to measure the annual return on a given investment and to compare different investment opportunities.

Junior mortgage. Any mortgage secondary to or of lesser priority than a first mortgage.

Land bank. An accumulation of land held for future use.

Land grant. A gift of public land to a state or local government, corporation, or individual.

Land residual valuation. An appraisal technique to determine land value by first calculating the value of a current or proposed development and then deducting the total cost of the current or proposed improvements including a developer's profit. It attributes any additional value to the land itself.

Landlord. An owner of leased real estate.

Lease. An agreement by which an owner of real property (lessor) gives the right of possession to another (lessee), for a specified period of time (term), for a specified consideration (rent), and under certain conditions.

Lease with option to purchase. A lease under which the lessee has the right to purchase the property. The price and terms of the purchase or the procedure for establishing the price must be set forth for the option to be valid. The option may run for the length for the lease or for only a portion of the lease period.

Limited partner. Contributor of capital to a limited partnership, who does not participate in running the business and is liable only up to the amount of his or her contributed capital.

Listing. An agreement between an owner of real property and a real estate agent, whereby the agent agrees to attempt to secure a buyer or tenant for a specific property at a certain price and terms, in return for a fee or commission if the transaction is consummated.

Listing agent. A real estate agent obtaining a listing (see above) from the seller, but who may or may not actually sell the property.

Load factor. (1) The ratio of rentable to usable space in a building. It can serve as a measure of design efficiency. (2) The amount of weight per square foot that the floor can support.

Loan coverage ratio. The ratio of the annual cash flow from operations to the carrying cost of the debt. Lenders use it as a measure of security for the loan.

Loan origination fee. A one-time fee charged by the lender for making or committing to make a loan.

Loan servicing. The bookkeeping, monitoring, and collection of a loan. It may be done by the lender or by a third party for the lender.

Loan to value or cost ratio. A key underwriting ratio, expressed as a percentage, derived by taking the amount of a loan and dividing by the value or projected selling price or the cost of real property. Usually, the higher the ratio, the greater the interest charged, because of the perceived greater risk.

Lot. Generally, any parcel of real property. Often refers to a portion in a subdivision.

Lot line. The boundary line of a lot.

Management fee. (1) The amount paid for property management calculated either as a percentage of collected revenues or as a fixed fee. (2) The amount paid for the overall management of an investment calculated as a percentage of value, cost, or income.

Master lease. A lease for an entire or a portion of a property that may be subdivided into subsequent leases.

Maturity. The time when a note becomes due in its entirety.

Mechanic's lien. A lien created by statute to secure priority of payment for the price or value of work performed and materials furnished in construction or repair of improvements to land and that which attaches to the land.

Minimum lot size. The smallest allowable lot size for development of a particular use, as stipulated by local zoning laws.

Minimum rental. A base rental in a lease. There may be additional charges for certain operating costs, a rise in the cost of living, or in the case of a lease for a retail store, a percentage of sales over a certain level.

Mini perm. A loan generally of five years to cover not only the construction period but also the initial years of rent-up and operation.

Month to month tenancy. A tenancy where tenant's occupancy can be terminated by either party on one month's notice, sometimes referred to as a "tenant at will." There may or may not be a written lease between the parties. Some jurisdictions may have additional restrictions or termination by a landlord.

Mortgage. (1) To hypothecate, or pledge as security, real property for the payment of a debt. The borrower (mortgagor) retains possession and use of the property. (2) The instrument by which real estate is hypothecated as security for the repayment of a loan.

Mortgage or loan broker. One who, for a fee, brings together a borrower and a lender and handles the necessary applications for the borrower to obtain a loan against real property.

Mortgage constant. The percentage relationship between the total of monthly principal and interest payments on a loan and the original face amount of the loan.

Mortgage term. The original or remaining number of years to maturity of a mortgage loan. If the mortgage term is less than the amortization term (see above), there will be some principal still outstanding at the loan's maturity. All such principal is due upon maturity in a lump-sum payment known as a "balloon payment."

Mortgagee. The party making a loan and receiving the mortgage payments. The loan is secured by a lien on the property.

Mortgagor. The party who borrows the money and grants the mortgage lien.

Negative cash flow. When the income from an investment property does not equal its expenses. The owner may have to come up with cash from other asset sources to meet these expenses.

Net lease. A lease requiring the tenant to pay, in addition to a fixed rent, certain specified expenses of the property leased, such as real estate taxes, insurance, or maintenance. Some refer to this arrangement as a "triple net lease."

Net present value. The calculation that discounts at a predescribed rate of return, generally on an annual basis, the net cash flows from operating and selling a property net of the discounted value of the original or future cash investments.

Nonconforming use. A use that violates zoning regulations or codes but is allowed to continue because it began before the zoning restriction was enacted.

Nonexclusive listing. A listing under which the real estate broker is given the right to sell a property, but the owner is not obligated to pay a commission if the property is sold directly or through another broker. Also called an "agency agreement."

Nonrecourse loan. A loan in which the lender's only recourse in the event of default is the security (property) and the borrower is not personally liable.

Notice to quit. A notice by a landlord to a tenant to vacate rented property for nonpayment of rent or another default. The notice for nonpayment may grant the borrower a specified time to cure the default.

Occupancy rate. (1) The ratio of actual income to the income if the property were fully rented. (2) The ratio of square footage leased to total rentable square footage. (3) The ratio of units rented to total number of units.

Open-space ratio. Ratio of space without buildings on a site to its total lot size. This ratio is often a zoning requirement.

Open-end fund. A commingled fund (see above) in which investors can invest or divest at a specified time, much like a stock mutual fund albeit less liquid. Its value is usually based on an independent appraisal.

Operating expenses. The costs of physically operating, managing, and providing services to an income-producing property. Such costs do not include any capital or financing expenditures.

Operating leverage. The disproportionate effect of increasing or decreasing cash flow from operations on the cash flow after financing. The effect is disproportionate because of the fixed level of financing expenses.

Opportunity fund. A pooled investment fund that buys distressed properties.

Option. A right given for consideration to purchase or lease property at an agreed-upon basis, within a specified time.

Option for additional space. An option as defined above to rent additional space in a particular property.

Origination fee. A fee paid to a lender for making a real estate loan, usually a percentage of the amount loaned.

Overage income or rental. Rental that exceeds the base rent. May be from a percentage of the tenant's sales (see percentage lease) or some other agreed-upon formula.

Overhang (for REIT). For REIT (see below), a large increase in the number of shares outstanding available for trading after initial public offering, or an acquisition in which certain shareholders are precluded from selling stock until a certain date.

Overhang (supply and demand). An oversupply of a particular property type in a particular market.

Override. A disproportionate share of the profits of a partnership, given to the general partner or the promoter under the terms of the partnership or venture agreement (see below).

Paper. A mortgage, deed of trust, or land contract that is given instead of cash. A seller would take "paper" if he or she received a mortgage, deed of trust, or land contract as part of the purchase price.

Parking ratio. The ratio of parking spaces to building area. For example: a rule of thumb for suburban office use may be three or four parking spaces per 1,000 square feet, and for apartment use, one or two parking spaces per unit.

Partnership agreement. A legal document that spells out all of the relationships among the partners to a deal.

Percentage lease. A lease, generally on a retail business property, using a percentage of the gross or net sales to determine the rent. There is usually a minimum or base rental.

Permanent mortgage. A mortgage for a long period of time, usually at least ten years. The mortgage is normally obtained at the end of construction and lease-up or the acquisition or refinancing of a seasoned property.

PITI. Principal, interest, real estate taxes, and insurance. The ratio of PITI to a buyer's total income is used by lenders as a test to determine a borrower's ability to repay a home loan.

Planning commission. A board of municipality that must approve or make recommendations in regard to proposed building projects, rezoning, or other related regulatory changes.

Plans. Architectural drawings related to a construction project. Depending on the level of detail, the plans may be called preliminary or conceptual design drawings or, if more comprehensive, detailed plans and specifications or working drawings.

Preliminary title report. A report showing the condition of lcgal title before a sale or loan transaction. At completion of the transaction, a title insurance policy, or final report is issued.

Prepayment penalty. A penalty under a note, mortgage, or deed of trust imposed if the loan is paid before it is due.

Prime tenant. The major tenant in a building. It may be necessary to have a prime tenant in order to obtain financing. The tenant may be considered "prime" because of its financial strength and/or because of the amount of space it occupies. (See also anchor tenant.)

Principal. (1) A person who has, as a result of managing an investment or directed legal authority, the right to act for an entity. (2) Amount of a debt, not including interest.

Profitability index. The ratio of the net present value of an investment to the total investment. It's sometimes a useful measure of comparison among various investment opportunities involving different capital contributions.

Property management. The branch of the real estate business that involves the management of property. Tasks may include accounting, bill paying, tenant relations, physical operations, rent collections, construction management, and leasing activities.

Property tax. Generally, a tax levied on either real or personal property. The amount of the tax is usually based on the assessed value for a particular property and the overall tax rate for similar properties in that community.

Purchase and sale agreement. An agreement between a buyer and seller of real property, setting forth the price and terms of the sale. When signed by both parties it is a binding contract.

Purchase money mortgage. A mortgage given from buyer to seller to secure all or a portion of the purchase price. It may or may not reflect the same terms that would be given by an independent lender.

Real estate. Land and anything permanently affixed to that land, such as buildings. It also includes fences and other attachments to the buildings, including light fixtures, plumbing and heating fixtures, and other items that would be personal property if not attached. The term is generally synonymous with "real property."

Real estate investment trust (REIT). A real estate mutual fund that does not pay corporate level tax on its income, provided (among other things) that 95 percent of net income is paid out in dividends. It sells shares of ownership and must invest primarily in real estate or mortgages. It must meet certain other requirements, including minimum number of shareholders, widely dispersed ownership, and asset and income tests.

Real estate owned (REO). Most commonly refers to property owned by a lender, especially a commercial bank, as a result of foreclosure on a mortgage or trust deed. This property is usually being held for sale by banks, as they are prohibited from investing in speculative real estate as equity owners.

Recourse. The right of the holder of a note secured by a mortgage or deed of trust to look not just to the property, but personally to other assets of the borrower or endorser for payment.

Red-lining. The outlining on a map of alleged high-risk areas for real estate loan purposes. This means lenders will not extend credit in these areas for real property loans, regardless of the qualifications of the applicant. Some states have passed laws against this practice. The use of a red pen or pencil for the outlining gave rise to the term.

Refinancing. Placing a new loan on a property to replace an existing loan without changing ownership.

Renewal option. The right of a tenant upon notice to renew or extend the term of a lease for a stated period of time and consideration.

Rent. Consideration paid for the occupancy and use of real property.

Rent control. A legally mandated limit on rental payments and/or increases in rental payments. It usually applies only to residential property.

Rentable area. The area for which rent can be charged. Generally it is the gross area of the full floor, less the area of all vertical penetrations (elevator shafts, stairwells, mechanical shafts, etc.) Rentable area includes the tenant's premises plus an allocation of the common areas directly benefiting the tenant, such as restrooms, first-floor lobby, common corridors, mechanical and janitor's rooms, and the elevator lobby on the tenant's floor.

Replacement cost. The current total cost to construct a building having the same utility as the subject building but using modern techniques and materials.

Reserve. A setting aside of funds, usually for indefinite contingencies such as future maintenance of structure or re-leasing costs, or for payment of certain operating costs such as insurance or real estate taxes.

Return on assets. A performance measure obtained by dividing annual cash flow from operations by total property cost. Used most often by lenders to make certain there is sufficient cash flow to service the debt. It is a static measure that looks at only one year of performance, without considering tax effects or the effects of any future sale or refinancing.

Return on equity. (1) A performance measure, also known as cash-on-cash return, derived by dividing the annual cash flow after financing (CFAF) by the initial equity. Because CFAF is a pretax measure, the return on equity calculation omits any tax effect. It also ignores the effect of any future sale of refinancing. The year used for measurement could be based on historical, current, or projected results. (2) The total return on equity over the term of ownership of a property.

Sale-leaseback. A sale and subsequent lease from the buyer back to the seller. Both transactions take place at the same time. It may be a way for the seller to obtain capital. The income tax consequences of such a transaction may be treated differently from its cash allocations.

Second mortgage. A mortgage that ranks after a first mortgage in priority. (See also junior mortgage.) Properties may have two, three, or more mortgages, deeds of trust, or land contracts as liens at the same time. Legal priority would determine whether they are called a first, second, or third (etc.) lien.

Security deposit. Commonly a deposit of money by a tenant to a landlord to secure performance of a written or oral agreement.

Shared appreciation. The allocation of increases in cash flow among various parties.

Site development. All improvements made to the land to enable construction of a building, such as grading, roads, and utilities.

Soft costs. Development costs for all items other than tangible improvements. Typical soft costs include architectural, engineering, and legal fees; property taxes, marketing, and leasing costs; and construction period interest.

Specifications. Detailed, written instructions, usually issued in conjunction with architectural drawings, defining how construction is to be performed.

Subchapter S-corporation. A corporation that is allowed by the Internal Revenue Code to be taxed as if it were a partnership. It must have thirty-five or fewer shareholders and meet several other requirements of the code. Thus a small corporation can distribute its income directly to shareholders and avoid the corporate income tax while enjoying the other advantages of the corporate form, such as a limited liability.

Sublease. A lease under which the sublessor assumes the obligations of all or part of a prior lease of the same property. The sublease may be different in terms from the original lease but cannot be for a longer term.

Syndication. An arrangement by which two or more people are assembled for the purpose of raising capital for purchasing real estate. Many properties are too expensive for an average investor to purchase alone. Therefore, in order to purchase such properties jointly, it is common for investors to combine their resources and establish a vehicle such as a corporation, cooperative, condominium, joint venture, or partnership.

Takeout loan. The "permanent" financing of real estate after completion of construction, generally for a term of ten years or longer. The loan replaces, or "takes out," the construction loan.

Tenant. A holder of property under a lease or other rental agreement.

Tenant improvement allowance (TI). The amount of money, usually measured per square foot, that the owner will pay for customizing and preparing the tenant's space at time of initial or subsequent leasing. It is generally a capital expenditure and must be amortized as such for tax purposes. TIs are subject to negotiations that may be affected by changing market conditions as well as by changing consumer preferences.

Term sheet. An outline of the conditions and arrangements to be specified in a formal contract, such as for a lease or loan.

Title. The evidence one has of right to possession of land, subject to deeds and restrictions of records.

Title insurance. Insurance against loss resulting from defects of title to a specifically described parcel of real property. Defects may relate to the fee (chain of title) or to encumbrances.

Title search. A review of all recorded documents and regulations affecting a specific piece of property to determine the present condition of title.

Transfer tax. An ad valorem tax on the transfer of real property based on the purchase price or amount of money changing hands. The amount of the tax varies by locality. Also called "documentary transfer tax."

Underlying financing. A mortgage, trust deed, or land contract with priority over another mortgage, trust deed, or land contract.

Unit. An individual apartment, condominium, or house in a larger property or subdivision, etc.

UPREIT. A type of REIT that does not own its properties directly but owns a controlling interest in a limited partnership that owns the REIT's real estate. Instead of receiving cash or REIT shares, property owners selling to the REIT take UPREIT "units," which are convertible into REIT shares, or the property is sold. Until converted, the shares are nonvoting.

Upset price. A term signifying the minimum price at which a property may be sold.

Usable area. The secured area occupied exclusively by the tenant within the tenant's leased space. The usable area, plus the tenant's proportionate share of common areas, results in rentable area upon which a per square foot rent is charged.

Vacancy allowance or factor. On a pro forma income statement, the amount of income estimated to be lost as a result of space for which no rent is paid. It may be based on historical, projected, or comparable rentals.

Variance. After a legal process, the change of certain zoning requirements for a specific property without changing the overall zoning for other properties in that district.

Working drawings. Drawings used to direct construction and showing all details, such as for structure, mechanical systems, electric, HVAC, plumbing, partitions, and other materials to be installed.

Zoning. The division of a city or county by legislative regulations into areas (zones), specifying the uses allowable for the real property in these areas, as well as height, setback, parking, and other restrictions.

Zoning ordinance. A law (generally at the city or county level) controlling the use of land and construction of improvements in a given area (zone).

ABOUT THE AUTHOR

MIKE BROWN is the co-founder and managing member of Red Fox Capital, a private commercial real estate investment fund for like-minded investors who want to pursue lucrative opportunities, diversify their risk, grow income, and create generational wealth. He brings more than twenty years of experience challenging investors to look beyond Wall Street by redefining the traditional investment industry through his innovative strategies.

After studying at the University of Georgia's Terry College of Business and the American Graduate School of Business in Switzerland, Mike completed the rigorous Certified Commercial Investment Member (CCIM) curriculum and his Masters in Commercial Property (MICP), a distinction that produces the top 5 percent commercial real estate practitioners in the world.

Mike is active on several banking advisory boards and serves as the development chairman for Veterans Moving Forward, a charity that provides service dogs to military veterans in need.

Made in United States
North Haven, CT
04 November 2026

21770786R00152